THE POLITICAL IMAGINATION

A Personal Response to Life, Literature and Politics

ALSO BY THE SAME AUTHOR

Fiction

A Time to Be Happy
This Time of Morning
Storm in Chandigarh
The Day in Shadow
Plans for Departure
Rich Like Us
Mistaken Identity
A Situation in New Delhi
Lesser Breeds

Non-Fiction

From Fear Set Free
Prison and Chocolate Cake
A Voice for Freedom
Indira Gandhi: Her Road to Power
Before Freedom: Nehru's Letters to his Sister, 1909-47
Jawaharlal Nehru: Civilizing a Savage World
Indira Gandhi: Tryst with Power
Point of View
Relationship
The Story of India's Freedom Movement

THE POLITICAL IMAGINATION

A Personal Response to Life, Literature and Politics

Nayantara Sahgal

HarperCollins *Publishers* India

First published in India by
HarperCollins *Publishers* in 2014
A-75, Sector 57, Noida, Uttar Pradesh 201301, India
www.harpercollins.co.in

2 4 6 8 10 9 7 5 3

P-ISBN: 978-93-5136-249-4
E-ISBN: 978-93-5136-250-0

The views and opinions expressed in this book are the author's own and the facts are as reported by her, and the publishers are not in any way liable for the same.

Typeset in 12.5/14.4 Centaur MT
By Saanvi Graphics Noida

Printed and bound at
Saurabh Printers Pvt.Ltd.

To my father
Ranjit Sitaram Pandit
Sanskrit scholar, sportsman and freedom fighter who died of his last imprisonment under British rule in 1944

CONTENTS

PART TWO

What Others Say

PART THREE

Fighting the Emergency

PART FOUR

My Homage to Three Greats

CONTENTS

PART FIVE

To, By and About Me

PART SIX

Miscellany

PART SEVEN

Reminders of a Cherished Friendship

Introduction: *The Politics of Imagination*

I am defining politics in a wider context as the atmosphere of the times we live in. I am saying that writing comes out of that particular atmosphere. Agatha Christie's wonderful detective fiction is a clear example. Her novels are not, by any stretch of the imagination, political, but they are firmly situated in the atmosphere of their time, which was imperialist and racist, and reflect its beliefs and point of view. Until empires packed up, the world was seen exclusively through a narrow Western canon. That began to change with countries coming into their own, and it further changed as migrant writing made its own impact.

Some would have us believe that migrant writing is apolitical because it emerges from what is now known as a global borderless world. This, of course, is not true. Art and literature have always crossed borders, though artists and writers did not. Being 'global' does not prevent migrant writing from faithfully reflecting its new situation, which is the result of its reactions to its adopted soil and surroundings. A writer's choice of subject, the way it is presented, and from what point of view, make writing a political act.

Nor is it true that the world is borderless. The nation state – with its history, geography, collective memory, and sense of identity – is very much with us. 'Global' has not erased the sense of national uniqueness. And contemporary literature across the world continues to be fashioned out of it.

If we take politics as such, it is just one more area of human experience for politics to draw on. The powerful novels and plays it has produced through the twentieth century – when political developments impacted human lives on a vast scale – have been the outcome of politically conscious imaginations. Writers have, through the cloistered act of writing, stepped into controversies, taken sides – not as polemics or propaganda – but through stories about the people who bear the brunt of the times they live in.

I hope I have, through my fiction and non-fiction, reflected the times I live in, and through this collection of my writing, I hope I have been able to reveal something of the politics of my own imagination.

NAYANTARA SAHGAL
Dehra Dun,
December 2013

PART ONE

The Personal and Political in Literature

Narrating the Political*

I've called my talk 'Narrating the Political' so first of all I should explain what I mean by political. We live in the atmosphere and conditions of a particular time and place. The world is what we see from where we stand. Writing comes out of that context – but in a hundred different ways. You and I may be part of the same era and environment, yet we may react to it very differently and write from radically different points of view. Our choice of subject, the way we describe it, and from what point of view, make writing a political act. Then, of course, there is politics as such. Earlier, the fallout of politics, including wars, did not break into private lives, so Jane Austen's characters could inhabit a private world untouched by the Napoleonic wars. But because political happenings have so intimately and directly affected private lives in the twentieth century as in no other century, politics has become one more area of human experience for imagination to draw on. The plays and poems and novels it has produced have not been about politics, they have been the outcome of politically conscious imaginations. Writers have, through the cloistered act of writing, stepped into controversies, taken sides, made it clear that this is right and that is wrong, not as polemics or propaganda but by fashioning the truth as they see it into the stuff of people's lives. Most often this has been a purely literary engagement with politics, but some, such as Wole Soyinka,

* Churchill College, Cambridge, 28 May 2011

have become political activists as well and suffered the consequences. Soyinka has spoken of having to survive twenty-one months of solitary confinement without human company and without books. In China, Liu Xiaobo is serving an eleven-year prison sentence and two other famous Chinese, Ai Weiwei (the design consultant for the birds nest stadium for the Beijing Olympics) and the famous writer, Liao Yiuri, are now under arrest. And the list is long of writers who have paid and are still paying a heavy price for the words they have chosen to put upon a page. Recently, Nadine Gordimer, a writer who has called herself unpolitical, has taken a political stand and, along with fellow writers, has drawn up a petition opposing the South African government's proposals to muzzle the media. Which makes me wonder if at some point in the life of even the most reclusive artist a time does not come when this rubicon has to be crossed. When artistic freedom is forbidden, the compulsions of life and literature become one and the same. Now, in this twenty-first century, the books I read by Afghan, Nigerian, Pakistani and Palestinian writers, apart from Indian, are as strongly political in theme or inspiration as Latin American or European fiction has been, or South African writing in the age of Apartheid. The literature of our time is saturated with the politics of our time as much as it is with any other aspect of life within us or around us.

In my own case, my political consciousness comes of the fact that I grew up in an occupied country. It was a paradoxical situation when the word 'occupied' applied only to the European countries invaded and occupied by Hitler and not the imperial occupation of countries in Asia and Africa. Empires did not see themselves as occupying powers. In this paradoxical situation I also grew up in a family committed to overthrowing British rule. Rebellion against the Raj meant imprisonment, deportation or death – and all this of course made politics an intensely personal and passionate involvement for my family and inseparable from our private life. There was, in fact, no such thing as a personal life that could be kept apart from the demands and duties of public life, with my elders having to spend years of their lives behind prison bars and my father dying of his last imprisonment under British rule. I don't remember a time when I was not politically aware of what was going on in my country or the world around us because we were an outward-looking, international-minded family. So that would be the short answer to why the 'political' dominated my imagination and became the material I drew on for my own writing.

A completer answer would be that in any case one has a need to make one's voice heard and to make oneself understood on one's own terms, and much more so when one is living in a world invented by others, as I was. My hometown in north India was this kind of invention. All the roads in Allahabad were named after Englishmen. In the best part of town, the shops sold English goods and catered to an English clientele. The two cinemas showed English and American films. Of course in school, I was taught English history, English language, English literature and English religion. And there was an imposing statue of Queen Victoria in the main park which for some reason was called Alfred Park and not Albert Park. No wonder all this led to a fight for freedom and to Allahabad becoming one of the centres of it! It is no exaggeration to say that as a child I felt like an unwanted alien, an outsider in my own hometown. Salman Rushdie has written about being haunted by a sense of loss when he revisited his old home in Bombay many years after becoming an expatriate. He felt that by going away he had been robbed of his whole Indian past. Well, as a child of rebels against British rule, I felt I was being robbed of my present, and that I was waiting for a future that might never arrive. And the present I was living in had nothing to do with me. It was shaped by imperial interests and attitudes and it took the Europe-centred point of view for granted as the only reality. Nothing was known about India except through Western eyes and interpretation. In such conditions, writing becomes a form of resistance. A famous example of the period is the history that Jawaharlal Nehru wrote in prison called *Glimpses of World History*. It was an alternative history from an Indian and Asian perspective, which was very different from the official imperial version. In a time of siege such as this was, when there was no other way of being heard, writing was an act of proclaiming one's very existence, apart from affirming one's own forbidden civilizational perspective. And an alternative literature came out of the same need. Fiction writers wrote their own diverse versions of India that were far removed from what others were writing about us. This is still happening because home-grown Indian writing chooses the themes relevant to it and is driven by very different concerns from Indian writing abroad. I think of these as two separate genres, each occupying its own space. There is, of course, a borderless world of literature to which all writing belongs, but as long as there are nations there are going to be national literatures. The link between soil and story makes for its own unique sensibility.

I started writing some years after independence – my first book, published in 1954, was autobiographical, and my first novel came out in 1958. The colonial period was over – at least as far as India was concerned – but 'post-colonial' had become the term for whatever came after, like a kind of Anno Domini from which all things have to be dated. Similarly, other terms, like the Middle East for example, and the Near East and Far East, have continued as common usage, dating from the time when these areas were so named according to their distance from Whitehall, and not according to their position on the map, by which the Middle East is geographically neither middle nor east, it is West Asia. As far as writing was concerned in the 1950s, India through Indian eyes was still waiting to arrive on the Western scene. An American survey around that time discovered that most Americans didn't know where India was on the map. And ignorance about India was profound. Orientalism was the order of the day – maybe it still is, in a subtler new incarnation to serve the market fundamentalism of the climate we now live in – but at that time it was upfront and unabashed. Let me give you a typical silly illustration of it. In the

1960s, I was on a lecture tour in America to promote a new book. I was wearing a sari and at one event during the question period, a woman in the audience said she was fascinated by my 'native costume' and would I show how I put it on. I replied that it was not my 'native costume', it was my clothes I was wearing and I couldn't take them off onstage. She seemed rather puzzled by my reply. Clothes were what people in the West wore. Other people wore 'native costumes'.

My writing took the only path it could take, that of my own experience; so my version of India had to be a country that took its democracy, its cultural pluralism and its secularism for granted. My novels, though I didn't plan them that way – I didn't plan them at all – turned out to be about the making of modern India. That was the dialogue I had heard debated and discussed all my life and it was as much a part of me as, I suppose, the Koran is for an orthodox Muslim or Genesis for a born-again Christian. Essentially this narrative celebrates an identity that is not something fixed and immutable, or mystical, or locked into race or religion or myth or ethnicity. It is a matter of choosing what you want to be and about the fact that there are universal human values that are not culture-specific, not Western or Eastern, but values we are all heir to. It has been exciting seeing the Arab uprisings demonstrating this today, and overturning stereotypical notions of identity. India made this point at independence when a devoutly religious country of many religions opted to become a secular republic with an atheist prime minister, without giving up any of its fervour for religion or tradition. I think my work found publishers and acceptance abroad, in spite of its lack of local colour, quaint customs, arranged marriages, maharajas and other exotica because there was a keen curiosity about this unusual new nation that had so firmly rejected stereotypical behaviour and declared itself in terms of its aspirations as a modern nation. It had also rejected the role others expected of it when it refused to line up with either superpower in the Cold War, and charted its own path as a non-aligned nation.

Most writers write about the same thing all their lives in different words and settings. The ongoing undercurrent in both my fiction and non-fiction has been this particular idea of India, and my stories have been about what went right and what went wrong after Independence, and whether we lived up to, or miserably failed to live up to the aspirations we set ourselves. If plenty hadn't gone wrong, I would not have had much material for storytelling. What went wrong, apart from providing drama for stories, was also a reminder that a nation, or what we think of as a national identity, is a work in progress, needing correction, revision, reworking – by the people themselves. Corruption has been hitting the headlines in India and just before I left India to come here, an anti-corruption campaign started by a well known seventy-three-year-old social activist had a tremendous spontaneous countrywide response from the public in the manner of Cairo's Tahrir Square phenomenon. It has led to a new bill being drafted for the next session of Parliament which we hope will make governance more transparent and accountable. Incidentally, all this rampant corruption, and the evils it has let loose in society, has made for two excellent Indian novels, one of which got the Booker Prize two or three years ago.

But let me give you some examples of how narrating the political works in my fiction. One of the things that went horribly wrong in democratic India was the two-year dictatorship called the Emergency that was imposed on us in the 1970s. I used it as the theme and background of my novel *Rich Like Us*. But in the telling, it becomes the story of how this shocking betrayal of democracy affects a number of lives, principally the lives of two women. One is an idealistic young Indian civil servant and the other is a beautiful ageing London cockney who marries an already married Punjabi businessman in the 1930s and comes to India to live as a co-wife. I wrote it several years after the Emergency because the Emergency itself played havoc with my life, cutting me off from earning a living. I had been writing political commentary for the newspapers critical of the government's slide towards authoriarianism and under censorship I could no longer write. A novel I had written suffered the same fate when the publisher who had contracted for it broke his contract, finding it dangerous to be associated with me. A moviemaker dropped a novel she had taken up for a film version for the same reason. I learned something about myself that other writers have learned in similar situations, that it is impossible to keep quiet when such things happen. Habeas corpus had been suspended and thousands had been arrested and jailed without trial, and I asked our national literary academy, the Sahitya Akademi of whose Advisory Board for English I was a member, to protest in writing about the assault on civil liberties and freedom of speech. They refused and I resigned. I then left the country for some months to avoid arrest and to write a political study of the prime minister, also to write for newspapers abroad and to explain what was happening in India in different forums. The plus side of this experience of dictatorship was that it awoke Indians to the need for civil liberties organizations. I served on the executive of one called People's Union for Civil Liberties during the 1980s.

Another unwelcome turn the country took which made for a novel was the rise of a militant Hinduism that believes in Hindu nationhood and in pickling and bottling India into a single Hindu monoculture. I felt the early rumblings of it and it gave me the surge of adrenaline I needed to start a new novel. When I actually started writing it, of course, it had nothing to do with Hindu fundamentalism, which was on the warpath in the 1980s and had long-lasting repercussions that led to the destruction of a historic mosque and later a massacre of Muslims in Gujarat. The rumble I felt simply acted as the trigger my imagination needed for a novel called *Mistaken Identity*, which was about none of those things and takes place in quite another historical setting – the 1920s. In that setting a feudal segment of India, loyal to British rule, lives the luxurious, leisured lifestyle of the landed aristocracy, quite oblivious to the revolutionary upheaval that is going on in the country, inspired by men as unlike as Lenin and Mahatma Gandhi. My favourite side of the story is of two remarkable women, a Hindu and a Muslim, both in purdah, who achieve liberation and flowering and fulfilment against all possible odds. The main story centres on Bhushan Singh, the handsome idle son of a Hindu landlord, who is obsessed with his search for his long-lost Muslim beloved. He looks like Rudolph Valentino, the great screen lover of the period, and he has absolutely no interest in politics. Basically he is a failed poet with a talent for ballroom dancing and for making himself charming. But one night in 1929 he gets taken off a train and dumped into jail along with a bunch of communists and a decrepit old Gandhian nationalist and all of them have to face trial for treason for plotting to overthrow the King Emperor. This is a time of industrial unrest and political agitation in the country and a number of famous conspiracy trials are taking place. On some nights, Bhushan Singh's interrogation in court goes on and on in his dreams. The prosecuting lawyer asks him what his religion is. Bhushan Singh, whose upbringing after all has made him a cultural mixture, says he is a Hindu Muslim. 'Your mother tongue?' demands the lawyer.

'My mother tongue is poetry but if you're going to finick about it, my mother tongue is Hindi and my father tongue is Urdu. My mother, illiterate though she is, hails from the Sanskrit script and my father from everything that hit us when Islam rode in. Let me assure you, Father wouldn't know Hindi letters from a crab's crawl. His tongue doesn't rise to the higher pillars of Hindi pronunciation. The glories of Sanskrit are Greek to him. The capital of his culture is Persia. Mother has forgotten how to read and she can't write. The Ganges Valley has other plans for its women.'

The exasperated lawyer says, 'This levity won't do. What are you? A Hindu or a Muslim?'

'I dream in both languages,' says Bhushan Singh in his dream, 'My diet, and therefore my digestion, are mostly Muslim. But my blood seems to circulate in Hindu fashion and my heart beats alternately to each.'

In Bhushan Singh, we see the sheer impossibility of prying two religions and two cultural heritages apart since they are housed in the same person – which is a metaphor for India as I see it. We are the result of mixture and cross-pollination, as I suspect everyone on earth is. There is no culture uninfluenced by others, and all talk of racial purity or cultural exclusiveness is, of course, sheer nonsense.

One of the most pervasive influences on my childhood environment was that of non-violence. My last novel *Lesser Breeds* is, among other things, about that amazing time when Indians used non-violence as a weapon of war, and Mahatma Gandhi gave the strangest command ever given to troops when he told his followers, 'If blood must be shed in this battle, let it be your own.' In the escalating violence of our own time, it reads like something that couldn't possibly have happened. I wanted to capture that period on the page before it vanished from the nation's memory altogether. I need not have worried about its vanishing. It has had a great revival in the Egyptian uprising, as it did decades ago in the American civil rights movement, and from time to time in those heroic men and women who have served as human shields against guns and tanks. And since non-violence refuses to die, one can hope that a time will come when enlightened citizens will refuse to subsidize arms build-ups, or to fund wars. *Lesser Breeds* is also about a young Indian girl who goes to college in the 1940s on what she thinks of as a far-off island called America, and becomes fascinated by the tribal customs of the islanders, especially their quaint tribal custom of Saturday night 'dating', and she makes a study of this rite and the strict rules governing the thus-far-and-no-further law that applies to kissing and cuddling on a date. She comes from an emancipated background herself, so she is intrigued by the fact that American women are so subservient to men, be they boyfriends or husbands or dress designers; and that the popular songs make things much worse by addling the most intelligent women's brains, and dumbing down their ambitions. It seemed to me it was time to stop being an anthropological specimen for others to study and to turn that time-worn scene around and give it another perspective.

Politics has been central to my non-fiction too, through autobiographical, literary and of course political commentary. My latest book is non-fiction. I've called it *Jawaharlal Nehru: Civilizing a Savage World*. It is a study of Nehru's role in building a new nation after more than a century of colonial stagnation, and the difficulties of doing so at the most dangerous time in history – the Cold War – when two lethally armed superpowers are fighting for control of the world. I think Nehru, who refused allegiance to both superpowers and rejected stereotypical positions for India, is particularly relevant today when West Asia is struggling out of many kinds of bondage and its people are trying to shape their identity according to their own light.

In closing – and because I'm here at the invitation of Churchill College – I'd like to share a story with you about Sir Winston Churchill that I've put into my book on Nehru. My mother, Vijaya Lakshmi Pandit, met him when she was India's high commissioner in Britain in the early 1950s and he was prime minister. At a lunch he had invited her to, he suddenly turned to her and said, 'We killed your husband, didn't we?' She was so taken aback at this admission from one who had been a sworn enemy of freedom for India that she didn't know what to say. But she recovered her composure and said, 'No. Every man lives to his appointed hour.' Churchill replied, 'That was nobly spoken.' The end of that story is that they became friends. Churchill was a man who chose his words with care. After he met and got to know Nehru at the Commonwealth Prime Ministers' Conference, he described him as the Light of Asia, and as one who had conquered mankind's two worst enemies, hate and fear. It was an astounding moving tribute from a diehard imperialist to his Indian adversary and it symbolized the historic turn the two countries had taken.

Tirur Festival*

Every year you gather here to celebrate literature in memory of the sixteenth-century poet and teacher who revolutionized the Malayalam language and brought the epics to the common people in a language they could understand. He made use of his creativity and his scholarship to expand the knowledge and enrich the lives of others. That he was drawn to the bhakti movement – to the belief that there is no need of priests and popes, no place for caste or class, no need of a middleman between man and God, no need even of a prescribed religion to lead one to God – speaks of the most profound understanding of religion and the most civilized instincts of humanity. Much that is happening in India today makes me wonder if we have the right to call ourselves civilized any more. So I am glad to have this opportunity to pay tribute to a saintly and civilized man. Long may his memory provide the example and inspiration that we so badly need today. I feel honoured to be here at this celebration of literature in his memory.

A celebration of literature is the same as saying we are here to celebrate diversity – in the shape of our many languages, our many voices, our many cultural differences, as well as the uniqueness of each individual vision. The best description I have heard of India's diversity came from the Hindi writer Nirmal Verma in an

---

* Keynote Kerala – 2 February 2011, Address at the invitation of Vasudevan Nair

interview he gave when he said that India has two great epics, the Ramayana and the Mahabharata, but also a third great epic which has no parallel anywhere, and that is the plural society made up of the coexisting cultures we call Indian. Personally I feel that if anything deserves to be labelled Brand India, it is this. And as a result of this, we have the most amazingly diverse literary scene in the world, whose scope and worth is yet to be recognized. Recently we have had authoritative opinions from abroad telling us there is nothing much worth reading in the Indian languages. Surprisingly, this opinion echoes the nineteenth-century sentiments of Macaulay and other British administrators who said that Indian literatures did not have the literary merit that was essential to uplifting the moral and mental standards of the natives to enable them to appreciate British rule. So only suitable selected English literary works were to be taught to the natives. The imperial power that occupied and controlled the land had to make sure of its control over minds as well. And what better way than through a carefully prescribed curriculum. In the same way, art and sculpture, religion and all aspects of culture had to be discounted and marginalized as being of no aesthetic or moral or intellectual value. All that was understandable when the West ruled the world. It is less understandable that we are still hearing echoes of that mindset.

The statement about Indian literature's unimportance reminds me of somewhat the same sort of attitude I came across when I was a college student in the United States many years ago. I was listening to a quiz programme on the radio where questions were put to an audience and the first person to raise his hand and give the right reply to each question got a big money prize. The last question carried the $64,000 prize and it was this: 'Is there any other Athens besides Athens, Ohio?' After a pin-drop silence one person replied, 'Athens, Greece.' He got huge applause as well as the huge prize. I think of that when I hear it said there is no Indian writing of worth except diasporic writing. It is like knowing there is an Athens in Ohio, but having to be told there is also an Athens in Greece. A more favourable remark we hear nowadays is that India's English writing has come of age, though it might be more accurate to say that the West's awareness of it has now come of age. But these are signs of the times we live in – times in which, as always, the powerful call the shots and the rest are expected to toe the line or fall by the wayside in the rush to what is known as globalization. And all this is further compounded by the fact that the market, and market value, rule every area of life, including sport and entertainment and literature, and value is decided accordingly.

But if Indian writing in the languages of India – the literature of an entire subcontinent – can be so casually dismissed in this fashion by judges based abroad, is it surprising when we ourselves have no proper knowledge or appreciation of our literary heritage and its offerings, for lack of translations? We have a literary establishment that doesn't need to outsource its judgement, one that sets its own professional standards for literary criticism. There are now more publishers, a growing number ofIndian literary awards and Indian judges for them, but writing in English still holds centre stage for want of translations. And translation – which itself is an art – is not of the consistently high level that writers wish for. I don't know the remedy for this but only a nationwide programme of translation from the original into other Indian languages as well as English can lift our literatures out of their regional isolation, first of all so that we can get to know each other. It is a fact that *we do not know each other,* because there is no way of knowing each other, no way of being intellectually and emotionally connected except by reading each other. And there is no way of correcting this lack except through translations. We have read the world's literatures through translations but we still have not read our own. There is a common literary heritage made of the sum of many parts that we have yet to discover. Our diversity is already apparent, not so the links and threads of a collective consciousness that bind us into a tapestry that we can then call Indian literature, just as Europe's diverse regions and languages can be said to add up to the edifice known as European or Western literature. This kind of development needs the cross-fertilization and cross-breeding of ideas and experiences that only reading and reacting to each other can bring about. Writing grows richer in contact with other writing. New narratives, new forms of expression and experimentation come into being in response to other forms and influences. The craft of writing is not cast in stone. It has no rules, or only rules that are meant to be broken if it is to unshackle itself from old laid-down patterns and invent new ways of expression. And for this to happen regional writing needs the stimulus of other regional writing, as all writing needs other writing to expand its awareness, to recharge language and revitalize itself. Literary acquaintance with our wider region should matter to us in this respect. Pakistan, Afghanistan, Bangladesh, Sri Lanka are producing fiction that grows out of our larger, older historical and cultural common ground. Though we live in a world that divides us, the world of letters shows us our common humanity. The freewheeling life of the imagination that we inhabit as writers has no borders and barriers. For a literary culture to grow and expand over India and Asia we need to meet and interact, carry on something of the kind of ongoing conversation that went on before, and for some years after, Independence in the Progressive Writers' Movement, which was a force in bringing writers, film-makers and other artists onto a common, originally an anti-imperialist, platform. Such luminaries as Faiz Ahmed Faiz belonged to it. And soon after Independence, a Progressive Artists' Group broke with traditional modes of painting and launched Indian painting into modern times. I don't know if there is anything similarly dynamic today that connects writers across India. Am I wrong in believing that our languages don't impact and influence each other?

I have talked of celebration, but I feel I am in mourning – for much that is happening in India and our neighbourhood. I am in mourning for Salman Taseer, the governor of Pakistan's Punjab, a man who has been murdered because he had the courage to oppose the law of blasphemy and tried to get a pardon for the Christian woman who is accused of blasphemy against Prophet Muhammad. I am in mourning for the mentality that rejoices at his murder. I am in mourning for the life sentence imposed on Binayak Sen, who has spent his career as a doctor among the tribal poor of Chhattisgarh, and used his position as vice-president of the People's Union for Civil Liberties (PUCL) to educate the people of Chhattisgarh about their human rights. The list is long of what needs to be mourned – above all the grim reality that three or four hundred million of us are desperately poor and their basic needs have not been met. At another level I mourn the fact that the democratic institutions established and meticulously served by Jawaharlal Nehru, Sardar Patel and that generation of leaders at the Centre and in the states – Parliament, the judiciary, the public services – have sunk into the spectacles of corruption and lawlessness we now see. And can anything be more unacceptable than that justice has been seen to serve the rich and powerful while ordinary people have no redress for the crimes committed against them? Could the terrible tragedy at Sabarimala have taken place if ordinary people received the attention and protection that is lavished on those who need it least? While I was writing my last book which has just been published – I called it *Jawaharlal Nehru: Civilizing a Savage World* – I felt fresh air blowing through my lungs, so different was governance then from the death and decay of standards we see today. I was reminded of higher standards when I came across an item in *The Hindu* of 11 January this year. The item was taken from 11 January 1961 and it said: 'Ram Krishna Dalmia, well-known industrialist, was sent to jail on January 10 to undergo two years' simple imprisonment on charges of criminal breach of trust of the funds of the Bharat Insurance Company.' Could this happen to a leading industrialist or politician or civil servant today? We have seen no sign of it so far.

In the midst of this gloom one exciting development taking place today is the resurrection of the world's oldest university, literally from its ashes. Nalanda University in Bihar was originally established in the early fifth century and utterly destroyed by the Afghan attack in 1193. but during its seven-hundred-year lifetime it flourished as a renowned Buddhist institution with a reputation that attracted scholars from all over Asia and as far west as Turkey, and taught, in addition to religion and philosophy, a vast range of subjects that included medicine, architecture, sculpture, astronomy and mathematics. It was famous in the ancient world for its spirit of intellectual and scientific inquiry, and for a great tradition of critical and scientific argument that refused to accept claims based merely on grounds of faith. How far removed we are from that enlightened mentality when we look at today's wishful and often hysterical claims over Ram Janmabhoomi and the temple madness it let loose over this country. Has the Indian brain shrunk through the centuries and become a pygmy brain incapable of rational argument, and is this why we now have to watch books, paintings and libraries vandalized, and artists and writers threatened by ignorant ruffians who cannot tolerate a dissenting point of view? These rampaging mobs who claim to be defending Hinduism need to recite the Gayatri mantra every day to remind themselves that Hinduism is about enlightenment. In such a climate we need a revived Nalanda University more than ever, and it is good news that its resurrection is now taking place under an interim governing body headed by Amartya Sen.

For those who live in societies like ours which are in need of change, can the writing of fiction be separated from 'political consciousness', by which I mean not politics as such but an awareness of the conditions we live in and the culture that the politics of any era produces? As opposed to migrant themes of exile, migrant problems of adjustment and the migrant philosophy of belonging nowhere and therefore belonging everywhere, we who are here belong here. India assails us from morning to night with its sights and sounds and smells, with its best and its worst, with what we draw strength from and take pride in, as well as what makes us despair. This is the scene we reckon with and cope with, the scene that involves our minds, our deepest feelings and all our senses; and so our writing will inevitably be different in substance and subject and style from Indian writing abroad. Diasporic and home-grown writing are two separate genres and each occupies its own space. Neither home-grown literature nor migrant literature can substitute for each other, but only those of us who live here, in this country in need of change, can change it – by what we write. Battles for change can only be fought on one's own soil and every battle begins by putting it into words. Nowhere is this more powerfully illustrated than in the writings of women, revealing how women have related to a society that has almost outlawed them as human beings. The most stirring example that comes to mind is Mahashweta Devi's extraordinary stories. I doubt if the combined brutality of tradition, religion, social conditions and the tyranny of politics and gender have ever been brought to bear on a woman's life with such shocking impact as in her fiction. Her storytelling makes literature a form of activism. Such writing also becomes an ethical activity that leaves us in no doubt about good and evil, right and wrong. Writing is an intensely private occupation but a great writer becomes a public voice. The writing of revolt and resistance that helped to deconstruct the British Empire is as needed today in making this nation fit for all Indians to live in. Staying put to bring about change is as true of life as of literature. We have seen a passionate commitment to change being demonstrated in politics by Aung Sang Su Kyi who has refused to quit her country to please the generals, though in exile she could have worked to some extent for her cause and lived a family life with her husband and sons. She chose instead to live as a prisoner in Myanmar, convinced that only by being there could she keep her struggle alive.

Fiction obviously has nothing to do with politics or economics or social and political conditions, only with the imagination that comes out of its own particular environment and creates stories that could come out of no other conditions. Nothing is more important in this globalized world, where the identity of all but the prevailing dominant culture is at risk, than that the local, the regional and the national be kept alive. As long as there are nations there will be national literature. What meaning can writing have if it is subsumed into a single point of view, if all writing arises out of the same broth? My own consciousness comes of growing up in Allahabad in a family involved in the fight for freedom, for whom everything revolved around the conviction that freedom must come first, before any such thing as a normal life could be lived. So life was not normal. Every aspect of it was heavily dominated by the national and international politics of the time and so politics became the material of my fiction and non-fiction. As a north Indian, cultural identity for me was a patchwork quilt of Indian and Western influences, of Hinduism, Islam, Buddhism, atheism and Christianity, and I have never been able to reduce it to anything simpler. To those who want to squash India into a Hindu monoculture, I have to say it would be un-Indian. It would be an artificial construct that I or millions of others would not be able to squeeze ourselves into. I have taken for granted my own fragmented self; my fiction and non-fiction come out of this awareness. My ongoing theme has been a secular one. I was writing *Mistaken Identity* at a time when Hindutva had begun the militant march that eventually erupted into the destruction of the Babri mosque, and this novel must have been my response to the change of political atmosphere, and to what I feared was coming. Non-violence has been another concern of mine and I paid tribute to it in my last novel *Lesser Breeds* which now reads more like an epitaph to a unique lost period in our recent history.

I have been talking about reading each other. A Tehelka survey some months ago found that people still read, books are still bought, but the ones that sell best are 'how to' books – how to make money, how to be a success in life and so on. Most Indians are young and if this is what 'reading' means to them, then the twenty-first century will be one in which Indians too will have to be reminded that there is an Athens in Greece besides the Athens in Ohio. I hope literary festivals like this one will prevent that spectre of a frightening intellectual decline overtaking us, and that literary festivals like this one will keep literature alive.

The Importance of Strangers*

You invited me to speak, with the suggestion that I could talk about my family and my writing with reference to the theme of this conference, which sets out (in your words) 'to explore the extent to which Britain was a dynamic contact zone, a crucible for the evolution of global modernities'. So that is what I've tried to do, and I am starting with the suggestion that this evolution was a two-way process, producing change on both sides. It seems to me that as individuals and as nationalities we are all the result of encounters with others, and of the outside influences, visible and invisible, that have been brought to bear on what we call home. There is no end to our involvement with strangers and the debt we owe them, or the extent to which we in turn impact them. The fallout of change works both ways. Neither side is ever the same again. The impact of Britain on India and of India on Britain was a result of this kind of encounter. When there were empires and the West considered itself The World, it was the empire's stamp on its colonies that was taken for granted – the reverse traffic would not have been conceivable in an era when inequality was the order of the day, and influence and impact were seen as flowing from the ruling race to the ruled. But of course it has been a two-way

* Keynote Address at the Conference on 'Bharat–Britain: South Asians Making Britain, 1870–1950', 13 September 2010

traffic, and it was happening all the while, but not acknowledged as such – as, for instance, in the case of the bond between Queen Victoria and her Indian munshi which was a mutual relationship at a human level, if not an equal one, long before any such thing was in sight on the subcontinent. Victoria seems to have been ahead of her contemporaries in her lack of prejudice.

Personally I am fascinated by the question of encounters and what they make of us. I dedicated a novel I wrote called *Rich Like Us*: 'To the Indo-British relationship and what its sharers have learned from it'. Its chief character, Rose, is a beautiful London cockney who meets Ram, a Punjabi businessman, in London in the early 1930s, falls headlong in love with him and marries him, though he is already married and has a son. Rose is intrepid enough and in love enough to cross an ocean to an unknown country and live in India as a co-wife. In the story Rose and India affect each other. For Rose, there is the cultural and emotional confusion and frustration of being a co-wife, there are her responses to political developments, including the national movement for independence which is in full swing, and her general outreach to all things Indian in contrast to her anglicized Indian husband who is a bit of a British stooge and does not have half her guts, her sterling human qualities, her curiosity or her sense of adventure. There is also a possible subtext – which wrote itself into the book and which I was unaware of while I was writing it – that Rose's fresh unbiased approach to India and vice versa may have been possible because she was not English upper-crust. At a time when race and class distinctions ruled the scene, she was of humble origins, though white, and maybe this is why she found it natural to identify with Indians as people, and not as a race apart, and to understand their political aspirations which imperial policy and the vested interests of the white ruling class opposed. One way of looking at the novel is that the strangers who cross our path, whether as individuals or as a slice of history, leave their indelible imprint on the persons or nation we become. We are the consequence of connection and involvement. And this has been a kind of ongoing refrain in my fiction. I believe in the importance of strangers.

Apart from my fiction, there has been the live experience of my own family in this regard, starting with my maternal grandfather, Motilal Nehru. The Indo-British encounter was countrywide and took place at different levels to a greater or lesser extent, but my family's experience of it is the one I know about, one that illustrates the changing course it took over three generations, from my grandfather's down to my own. The brief background to it is that Motilal Nehru's father was a police officer in Delhi serving the last Mughal emperor at the time of the Mutiny in 1857. He fled the city with his family along with thousands of others fleeing British vengeance when the British retook Delhi from the mutineers and sacked the city. Motilal Nehru was born posthumously in 1861. He was brought up by one of his two older brothers and he read only Arabic and Persian until he was twelve years old. He came late to English. With neither money nor connections he laboured long and hard to set himself up in the legal profession, and worked at a furious pace to support his own family and his brother's seven children, of whom he took charge when he himself was only twenty-six years old and their father died.

By the first decade of the twentieth century, Motilal had a nationwide reputation and had made a fortune at the Allahabad Bar. He was owner of a palatial mansion, playing host to the most eminent Indians and Englishmen of his generation. In 1899 he had taken his first trip to Europe and had refused to go through a purification ceremony on his return as caste and custom required. This had nothing to do with the transforming winds that were blowing from the West, just as his secularism was not West-inspired but ingrained in him as integral to his north Indian Hindu-Muslim culture. He had no patience with the Hindu revival movement and its 'Back to the Vedas' call. He was interested in moving forward. And being a self-made success, he made his own rules and refused to put up with the humbug of meaningless ritual. He was excommunicated by the orthodox but his example paved the way for young Kashmiri men of his community to defy orthodoxy, travel abroad and refuse to do penance on their return. Motilal's relationship with the West, specifically with Britain, had a much bigger scope and significance.

Britain ruled India and in that high noon of the Empire this was an unchallenged fact. It had its advantages and disadvantages. There were new masters, their language to be mastered, their laws to be obeyed. The racial divide was absolute and social segregation was the norm. White society lived in its own enclaves. There were permissible limits within which Indians could rise. They were not allowed to train as officers for the Indian army or rise to executive positions in the administration. When, in 1882, an Indian was appointed district magistrate for the first time, there was a cry of alarm. The English-owned paper, *The Pioneer*, warned it was 'premature to put natives in charge of districts'. Whatever the clamps and cautions of policy, there was no stopping the blast of ideas and fashions from abroad, from political thought and advances in science to sport, food, clothes and hairstyles. They found fertile soil in a generation of Indian men educated in English history, language and literature. But modernity stayed male. For the most part, westernization was kept within limits. It remained at a safe distance from the sanctum of private life and did not cross the threshold to impinge on the cuisine or culture or pastimes of home and the women of the family. Motilal became a spectacular exception in this regard. He brought the British impact home and established it in family life. He did this with the zest and energy he brought to everything he did, whether it was his drive to the top of his profession or to his gourmet enjoyment of food and drink and life in general. The household remained anchored in its Indian roots, but the home for all practical purposes became an English upper-class home, the first house in Allahabad to have flush toilets, electric light and an indoor swimming pool, and the first to have, besides its stable of horses and carriages, motor cars ordered from

England. There were English tutors for Motilal's son, an English governess for his daughters, and clothes for himself tailored in Savile Row. Motilal was no socialist or republican. On the occasion of the royal visit to India in 1911, he 'received the command of His Gracious Majesty King Emperor George V to be in attendance at Delhi', and ordered a complete elaborate court outfit at Poole's of London. He and his family travelled to Delhi as guests of the lieutenant governor of the province in his special train and stayed in the governor's camp in Delhi. British officialdom had a high opinion of Motilal's professional accomplishments, felt at home with his elegant westernized lifestyle and enjoyed his lavish hospitality. But it was his personality and independent spirit that commanded their respect as an equal. A British visitor to his home remarked of him that wherever he sat became the head of the table. At a time when park benches and railway compartments had 'Europeans Only' signs, the British chief justice of the high court offered to propose Motilal's name for membership of the exclusively European Allahabad Club – an offer that Motilal declined.

There was no conflict in Motilal's mind between his patriotic pride and the English lifestyle and outlook he had made his own, nor any question of either-or, or of thus-far-and-no-further. He perceived Britain as India's way forward and British rule itself as the dynamic that would carry India to greater self-rule. It was an opinion he had in common with leading figures of the Indian intelligentsia, only being the man he was, who did nothing by halves, he took this conviction to its logical conclusion when he plunged his whole family into the crucible of change. Like a number of his famous contemporaries he believed that Britain's unjust policies in India were not the result of British rule but of 'un-British' rule which was a betrayal of Britain's own high ideals. *Poverty and Un-British Rule in India* was the title of a book by Dadabhai Naoroji, published in 1902. This collection of Naoroji's speeches was a detailed indictment of Britain for keeping India impoverished by bleeding her for Britain's wars, otherwise draining her of her resources and not allowing Indians more control of their own affairs. But he blamed all this on what he called 'the present dishonourable un-British system of government'. He predicted a 'glorious future for Britain and India ... if the British people will awaken to their duty, will be true to their British instincts of fair play and justice, and will insist upon the "faithful and conscientious fulfillment" of all their great and solemn promises and pledges.' He tried to educate Victorian England through the London Indian Society he had founded in 1865 about what needed to be done to address Indian grievances. On his election to the House of Commons in 1902 as a Liberal member, Naoroji said, 'We hope to enjoy the same freedom, the same strong institutions which you in this country enjoy. We claim them as our birthright as British subjects.' In 1897, Sankaran Nair addressing the Indian National Congress had said it was 'impossible to argue a man into slavery in the English language'. And Gokhale had called for 'a nobler imperialism' to replace 'narrower imperialism'. In 1907, Motilal Nehru, in a long presidential address to the Allahabad Conference, praised England, acknowledged India's debt to her and said, 'I firmly believe that (John Bull) means well – it is not in his nature to mean ill. This is a belief that is not confined to myself alone ... and will be readily endorsed by those who have seen and known John Bull at home. It takes him rather long to comprehend the situation, but when he does see things plainly, he does his plain duty, and there is no power on earth – no, not even his kith and kin in this country or elsewhere – that can successfully resist his mighty will.' It was a time of trust in Britain, tremendous hope and optimism that what was considered true Britishness would prevail, and Indian demands for political reform and for larger Indian participation in policy and governance would be granted. At the turn of the century, what Indians were seeking, in the words of Dadabhai Naoroji – the most respected voice of Indian nationalism – was 'self-government under British paramountcy or true British citizenship'. It was the belief that Britain would hold good on this promise that led Gandhi – later

Mahatma – to organize Indian volunteer ambulances for Britain's Zulu war and the Boer War in South Africa, and Indian opinion to rally round Britain in the First World War. This was the mood and atmosphere in which India's first organized political party – the Indian National Congress – had been launched in 1885 by a retired British civil servant, Allan Octavian Hume, to channelize and promote India's rising expectations along the lines of a loyal Opposition to His Majesty's Government. Had these moderate ambitions been realized at that moment in time, history would have proceeded very differently. The modernizing impact of Western ideas was proving to be a two-edged sword. Having created a demand for change, it expected the demand to be heard and fulfilled.

Hume was an ardent champion – and there were others among English men and women – of the Indian desire for rapid progress towards self-government, not then conceived as outright independence. The presence of such opinion among the English themselves strengthened India's faith in Britain's intentions. These Englishmen were visible proof, as it were, that there was a meeting of minds on the crucial issue and that the day would soon come when 'British subject' and 'equal status' would mean the same thing. Indians and their English supporters shared the conviction that reform would empower Indians by gradual stages, as it had empowered the English people themselves in slow stages through Acts of Parliament.

While Motilal in India was describing himself as more moderate than the Moderates in the Congress – a party he took little interest in since his career took all his time – his son, at school in England, was reading Trevelyan's book on Garibaldi, dreaming of heroic deeds and 'of how sword in hand I would fight for India and help in freeing her'. Jawaharlal Nehru was not at a school for raving revolutionaries. He was at Harrow which, along with Eton, had educated nearly every future viceroy of India from 1884 to 1947. Later, from Cambridge, Jawaharlal wrote to his father of his attraction for Sinn Fein. 'The policy is not to beg for favours,' he wrote, 'but to wrest them.' His sympathies were also with the Extremists at home. 'As regards John Bull's good faith I have not so much confidence in him as you have ...' he wrote. Indian nationalism was being bred not on Indian soil but on the ground that had bred Britain's empire builders. Britain, all unwitting, was serving as the 'dynamic zone' for breeding rebellion against herself. It was the British-educated Jawaharlal who swept his moderate father and entire family into the Gandhi-led fight against British rule and it was under Jawaharlal Nehru's leadership that the Indian National Congress in 1929 abandoned all compromise and announced independence as its goal. A psychological turning point had come with the massacre at Jallianwala Bagh ten years earlier, putting an end to the faith in 'true Britishness'. It was seen that law and order, English education, roads, railways and telegraph wires were signposts of a modernity that did not include racial equality. Winston Churchill immortalized the imperial mindset during the Second World War when he said that the Atlantic Charter's reference to freedom for 'all men' meant all Europeans under Nazi occupation, and not others under foreign occupation.

In 1921, when Motilal's family, men and women, joined Mahatma Gandhi, Motilal's home, known for its British lifestyle and its legendary luxury and never known for half measures, made a blazing bonfire of its British goods and boycotted them thereafter. The family wore coarse handspun khadi from then on and entered a harsh and austere regime of civil disobedience and jail sentences.

Motilal Nehru's transformation from loyal subject of the King Emperor to outright rebel astounded his English friends. An English journal described their shock as resembling that of 'a fond Edwardian father whose delightful daughter became a suffragette and broke his windows'. When Gandhi started his Salt March to Dandi in 1930, Motilal donated his palatial mansion to the Congress party and moved into a smaller house he had built on the estate. All-out war, albeit non-violent war, had been declared against the British government and there was no looking back. The passion and dedication of my elders made me long to grow up quickly so that I too could go to jail. Meanwhile, we children were not allowed to cry in front of the police when they came to arrest our parents. Family discipline called for, of all things, a British-style 'stiff upper lip'.

I have never felt as alien in any foreign country as I did in my own hometown as a child – where all the roads were named after Englishmen, the park had a statue of Queen Victoria and the best shops stocked English goods for an English clientele. What saved one from deep distress was the humour of the situation. The thing about racial superiority is that it has to be upheld round the clock. Not for a moment can vigilance be relaxed, and upholding British prestige among the natives had its hilarious aspects. Love, for instance, was a hopeless dilemma in novels and movies of the period if the English heroine discovered that the Englishman she had fallen in love with in some outpost of the Empire was suspected of having a drop or oriental blood. In a novel I read as a child, a tragic ending was dramatically averted in the last chapter when it was discovered that the drop of blood was Spanish. In the movies, Charles Laughton as Henry VIII could not be shown gnawing at huge chunks of meat at dinner. An English monarch could not be seen eating with his fingers and displaying gross table manners. The censors deleted that scene for viewing in India. A film about the adulterous love affair of Lord Nelson with Emma Hamilton, originally titled *That Hamilton Woman* was more decorously retitled *Lady Hamilton*. The natives meanwhile got their own back with jokes about the white sahibs and memsahibs. Some of these were hilarious examples of the inroads that our two languages – Hindi and English – had made into each other. The master–servant relationship, lopsided though it was, did allow for interaction of a limited kind between ruler and ruled. Otherwise, the unbridgeable gulf between the English and the people they ruled was a growing, glaring fact.

E.M. Forster had taken a penetrating look at it in his *Passage to India.* I was reminded of the assumption of white ownership and arrogance I had been humiliatingly aware of as a child, when years later I watched Paul Scott's *Jewel in the Crown* on TV. I recalled that, as children, my friends and I had invented tortures for Mr Amory, then Secretary of State for India. Our favourite one was tying him up in a desert with water just out of reach.

The family I grew up in was committed to overthrow British rule, but there was no such commitment to overthrow Winnie the Pooh, Agatha Christie, P.G. Wodehouse or the classics of English literature, and there was nothing against eating shepherd's pie or custard pudding for dinner. Agatha Christie and P.G. Wodehouse were also favourites of the late Jyoti Basu, who became a communist in England in 1940 and after Independence headed communist governments in West Bengal for twenty-three years. His allegiance to Karl Marx notwithstanding, it was Hercule Poirot and Bertie Wooster who eased his burdens of office. Nor was there a contradiction in any of this. Inheritance is many-sided and takes many forms.

My grandfather had seen Britain as the way forward and there was much about Britain that the Indian imagination, though it was in revolt against British rule, continued to hold in respect. Above all, it admired the way the British governed themselves, and its admiration for the steel of British character, so evident under attack during the Second World War, was unbounded. I remember that my father who had been three times imprisoned during British rule, who was to die in 1944 of his last imprisonment, mourned when Britain came under bombardment during the blitz, and when Hitler's army marched into Paris. During the struggle for freedom, friends and allies had been gained in Britain and in many parts of the world for India's independence. Nothing had made so global an impact or so stirred the world's conscience in modern times as India's war without violence. And there were Englishmen and women, many Quakers among them, with whom we could join forces and forge global links in common causes that transcended nationality at a time when the British government was silent on fascism in Italy and Nazism in Germany. There is a wonderful picture of Jawaharlal Nehru in my latest book on him, speaking, it appears, with great passion at a rally in Trafalgar Square during the Spanish Civil War. He also went to Barcelona with Krishna Menon, then head of the India League in London, to assess the situation for himself.

A few years after Independence, Winston Churchill, as prime minister, asked my mother, Vijaya Lakshmi Pandit, what in her opinion had been Britain's biggest mistake in India, and she replied segregation – the unofficial apartheid that had made it impossible for the communities to meet and get to know each other on an equal basis. It had certainly made it impossible for Churchill to regard Jawaharlal Nehru as anything but a traitor and an enemy. When he finally met Nehru at the first Commonwealth Prime Ministers' Conference in London, he was so deeply impressed by his personality and his influential role in the conference that he called him the Light of Asia. He also told my mother that her brother had conquered mankind's two greatest enemies – hate and fear. This was a remarkable tribute and a remarkable reversal of perception – the result of an Indian impact on Britain made by the Indian who had spent ten years as a prisoner of the British on the Englishman who had vowed never to dissolve the British Empire. Virtual apartheid, which is the denial of human equality, had prevented a unique encounter from taking place many years earlier between these two men, one that might have made the transfer of power a much earlier routine event and not the tortured and terrible saga it later became.

Nehru never had the categorical one-dimensional approach to England that Churchill had had to India. Student years spent abroad do not necessarily make a foreign country feel like home, but given his westernized upbringing, England was, in a sense, a continuation of India for Nehru and not the complete 'elsewhere' it might otherwise have been. Returning to England after a vacation in India, he had written to his father in October 1908, 'The familiar sights and sounds had quite an exhilarating effect on me.' He remained aware of, and indebted to, his English inheritance. In essence, he regarded India's history as richly layered, every layer of it integral to the sort of people Indians had become. As prime minister, anticipating his first visit to America in 1949, he wrote to his sister, my mother, who was then the Indian ambassador to the United States: 'Which facet of myself should I put before the American public – the Indian or the European, for after all I have that European or English side also ...' The emotional impact of inheritance is a diverse and 'dynamic zone' of its own that has no measure. I saw this impact in reverse as I watched Attenborough's film *Gandhi* and Ken Griffith's one-man film portrayal of Nehru. Both Attenborough and Griffith seemed to me intellectually and emotionally, besides being artistically, involved with their subjects, and with a whole slice of history. They were not Englishmen surveying the scene as outsiders. A point is reached in the experience of 'encounter' when each has become part of that shared experience.

I've made no study of how historical encounters in other cases resolve themselves or how other countries reckon with the legacies of outside influences. The story goes that a European journalist asked Deng Xiao Ping if the French Revolution had influenced the Chinese revolution, and Deng Xiao Ping replied: 'Too soon to tell.' From that awesome Chinese perspective, it may well be too soon to assess Britain's impact on India or the reverse. But we do know that when the parting of the ways came in 1947, instead of tearing the past out by the roots and throwing it away, India gave this embattled relationship yet another turn by opting to build on what she chose to retain of the British connection: a commitment to parliamentary democracy and related institutions. India also made short work of the foreignness of the English language by declaring English to be one more Indian language. And in acknowledgement of the most recent layer of Indian history, she invited the last British viceroy to become the first governor general of free India.

To get back to family, the transfer of power forged bonds of friendship and affection between my rebel family and the last viceroy's that continue to this day. It would seem the wheel had turned full circle since Motilal Nehru's robust involvement with Britain began.

Climate Change or Is the World Becoming Flat Again?*

I thought hard about what I should say to this illustrious company, in this historic city, at the start of a new year, and on the occasion of a very special kind of festival which is multilingual and multi-textured, as it includes the music, arts and crafts of India along with writing from India and abroad. But above all, it is about literature, so what can I say at this particular moment in time about literature? And it seems obvious to me that I must talk about climate change – not of course about global warming but about the way the mental and emotional climate we are living in affects those who write. So I am calling this talk Climate Change or Is The World Becoming Flat Again? – by which I mean a limited world whose people see thus far and no further.

We are here to celebrate literature which is the same as saying we are here to celebrate diversity – the importance of being different from each other, the value of each individual vision. Literature means many voices. As writers, we project our unique points of view. As readers, other writers show us there are others besides ourselves – other visions, other values, other ways of living and thinking. India has always seemed to me to be a good place to have a celebration of many voices. One of my favourite writers, Gabriel

* Inaugural address at Jaipur Literature Festival, 23 January 2008

Garcia Marquez, once called his continent a microcosm of the human race, and this subcontinent is pretty much the same kind of mix and muddle of races and cultures. In India we have a plurality of religions and languages thrown in besides. Racial purity, a single book, a single way of life, one prescription for solving the world's problems, would seem absurd to us here, a fantasy we would never consider. I'd like to say we never will. Instead, I have to say that diversity, here as in many parts of the world, is under attack. And because diversity is at the very heart, the very meaning of literature, I have wondered how creativity in life and literature is going to be affected – is already being affected – by the relentless drive towards sameness that is being laid down by religious fundamentalisms on the one hand, and on the other hand by the increasingly look-alike-think-alike world that globalization based on marketization is producing.

I've used the word celebration, but recent events have given us more cause to mourn than to celebrate. Next door to us in Pakistan Benazir Bhutto has been murdered because there are those the world over who believe that assassination is the way to deal with opposition. Next door to us again, in Bangladesh, the writer Taslima Nasreen has had to flee her country because neither her life nor her writing are safe there. Here in India, Muslim hardliners have forced her to withdraw what they call offending passages from one of her books. Here too the painter Hussain has been driven into exile to escape the wrath of Hindu fundamentalists who accuse him of insulting their religious sentiments. Just recently, extremists threatened to vandalize an exhibition of his held in Delhi and smashed the NDTV office in Ahmedabad for including his name in a poll they conducted. And not long ago a valuable archive in Pune was attacked and a manuscript burned because it supposedly hurt Maratha sentiments. We in India can no longer say, 'It can't happen here.' In postmodern India all this is happening. And it has happened with religious sanction and state sanction.

And what is happening elsewhere is as disturbing. In Turkey a misguided nationalism is persecuting its writers, including one who decried the ferocious ethnic cleansing of its Armenian population. In the West, famous and admired writers have supported the war against Iraq and have had nothing to say about the invasion, occupation and plunder of a sovereign nation or what such lawless behaviour has done to international law. Famous and admired writers have fallen into the trap of seeing Islam as an enemy and Muslims as terrorists, forgetting others who unleash havoc and terror in parts of the world. And Muslim-phobia has made young and old Asian immigrants in the West fear being targeted as terrorists. There seems to be no clarity about how to deal with multiculturism – how to cope, what to allow, what to ban. And this sometimes results in well-intentioned governments working with extremist and obscurantist opinion among Asians, in the mistaken notion that they are the real representatives of their culture – not realizing that there is a very different and much broader framework to Asian identity and aspiration. India has shown that a multicultural society where religions are valued and practised can be based on a secular ideal. Multiculturism is nothing new to the world. Empires, including the Ottoman, lived with it. Until recently Yugoslavia and the Soviet Union practised it. And today many societies are experiencing aspects of it. Cultures need other cultures to recharge and revitalize themselves. Others who are not the least like ourselves have to be admitted, accepted, understood. It is the outsider who crosses our path who brings the fresh air and excitement of new ideas and new vistas our way. Languages run into each other and invigourate each other. New forms of expression come into being in response to other forms and feelings and ideas. But need I say more when we look at the exhilarating effect of immigrant writing on English literature and the intoxicating things that happen when vastly different art forms and traditions come together? Some years ago at a concert in London I heard Yehudi Menuhin and Ravi Shankar perform together. I would never have believed that a violin and a sitar could combine in a duet and that this unlikely combine could make such music happen. It was a magical and unforgettable experience. And more of this is now happening in cinema, the theatre and other art forms.

Postmodern is also connected in my mind with a climate ruled by commercialism. The other day I was interested to read that no less likely a person than the former attorney general of the United States had called globalization based on economic power, consumerism and materialism deadlier than armed conflict, because the spread of sameness – the same technology, the same kind of entertainment, the same junk food, the same desire for the same endless toys – will wipe out the distinction between one culture and another. Ultimately whole areas of human experience and accumulations of human imagination will simply disappear. And if this is the process we are in, how are minds going to stay free and open in such a climate? The ruling theories and philosophies of any era shape its thinking and create its mindset. The things we believe in restrict our imaginations or set them free. The mindset of people who thought the world was flat was very different from those who knew it was round and could set out to explore the difference. What I'm afraid of is that the world is becoming flat again and we are getting locked into an either-or, we-and-they, black-and-white way of thinking, a shrunken, sterotyped, cliched world with no room in it for search, for shades of meaning or for adventures of ideas. And this is a condition for which the laid-down certainties of our time – whether religious or economic or violently nationalistic – are all responsible.

Writers used to react to and comment on such defining moments and developments – and this moment is as defining for our time as the difference between a flat and a round world once made. Writers stepped into controversy, took sides, said this is right and that is wrong Will this kind of involvement become unfashionable in the twenty-first century? There are those who argue that this is politics or this is economics and has nothing to do with literature, but when have politics and economics not been part of literature? What else are they but the conditions we live under, making us the kind of people we become? The politics of every century has affected private life, never more horrifyngly than in our own time. Pablo Neruda explained his transition from love poetry to political awareness in the words of a poem called 'Let Me Explain a Few Things', and I quote: 'You will ask: and where are the lilacs/ and the metaphysics petalled with poppies/ and the rain repeatedly spattering its words ... Come and see the blood in the streets/ Come and see the blood in the streets ...' Yet becoming politically aware didn't prevent him from writing odes to red wine and artichokes and onions, or lyrics to the body of his beloved. Neruda's poetry, his personal life and his politics were all one, as was the case with so many poets and novelists and playwrights in the twentieth century who also became – perhaps for that very reason – the most widely read writers of their time. Will the twenty-first century produce this breed? I don't say times mustn't change – only that we have to play a part in the changes, decide what direction change should take, influence it, not stand by and let it happen, for better or for worse.

Incidentally, I've been told by my daughter who is familiar with it that great things are happening in children's literature in Britain, that it is more varied and wonderful and profound than it has ever been. It has always been wonderful, from Alice in Wonderland on – one of my own favourite books is still *The Wind in the Willows* – but now it covers a wide range of ideas and emotions, from metaphysical questions to the heartbreak of divorce for children. It seems to have escaped being sucked into our confining climate and has created a climate of its own.

I'm probably more aware of the commercialism of our current book climate because it is so different from when I started writing. My first novel was published in 1958. No one then judged a manuscript by how many copies it would sell. Agents and editors had a part to play in recognizing quality and taking risks if need be to nurture it. Books of topical interest were important and there were plenty of them, but fiction was not a matter of topical interest or current fashion. I remember asking my editor at Alfred Knopf whether he thought a particular novel was 'timely' and he said they chose fiction for its timeless quality. And Victor Gollancz who published me in Britain had much the same attitude. Publishers considered themselves taste-makers, opinion-makers. Agents and editors did not intrude into the process of writing – at least I never had such an experience, never so much as a change of sentence. This came back to me very strongly when a few years ago a successful young Indian–American writer told me how beholden she was to her agent for the content, shape and structure of her novel. He had told her what to enlarge on, what to leave out, and generally decided how her product should be 'packaged' for the best effect. I don't know how typical this is – or whether it is necessary now that books and publishing are big business – but I am grateful that I made my start in times when nobody told me what or how to write, and before marketization and corporatization had taken over the arts. I even wrote novels with political backgrounds which were not in keeping with the general understanding of what India was all about – which was quaint customs, local colour, arranged marriages, maharajas and the like. But thanks to enlightened publishers I got published, sold and read.

Postmodernism has not led to post-nationalism. We are as far from becoming one world as we ever were – though we are a better-connected world. The nation state is very powerfully with us. But fortunately, a truly universal literature is growing out of a wealth of national literatures. India alone has ancient literatures among her many languages – and voices among them in prose and poetry that have never reached mainstream publication. Translation and world interest are at long last bringing at least some of these a wider readership and recognition that only Indian writing in English has enjoyed. The bond between soil and story remains a unique and irreplaceable one, coming as it does out of a people's own history and geography and collective consciousness. Strange as it may seem at a time when cross-cultural experience occupies centre stage on the literary scene and English is the dominant language, most of the world's people still stay put on their own soil and the writers among them write in their own language. I hope enterprising Indian publishers will bring the works of foreign writers to India through translation into Indian languages and that translations will flow both ways. That foreign, mainly, I think, British, writers choose to live and work here, just as a number of Indian writers live and work abroad, is testimony to the truth that literature knows no frontiers and an artist's country is the realm of his or her imagination.

As I've been talking I've had more uncertainties than answers in my mind. Perhaps you know the answers. But of one thing I am certain, that writers will write, whatever the odds, and I want to wish them safety and freedom in a new year of great writing.

Illusion and Reality*

I can only share with you some thoughts I have on the collection of islands and continents we call the world, which are the subject of this conference, and talk about some ideas that have governed this world and their effects on us, for it is my belief that writing comes as much out of this heritage as the heritage known as a literary tradition.

I have to speak personally and as an Indian. How else can one speak, except from one's own time, experience and position, with all the limitations that these impose? And when I say 'we' or 'us', I am referring to the people who lie more or less within the same general ambit of experience and share a somewhat similar outlook. And in these very broad general terms it seems to me that the 'we' I speak of are the people who live out scenarios that have been conceived elsewhere, and been directed from that elsewhere by other people. The real world we have been repeatedly told we live in has not been the one whose reality we could believe in. For us, it has been a stage set by others on which we have played the roles assigned to us.

The imperial era I was born into was a stage setting of this kind. Empire itself was no illusion. It was a fact of life, a businesslike arrangement that had divided up the globe into rulers and the ruled,

---

* Keynote Address at Association for Commonwealth Literature and Language Studies (ACLALS) Conference 'Islands and Continents' at Colombo on 14 August 1995

masters and slaves. Under this dispensation huge land masses with names and ancient civilizations of their own became quaintly known as Europe's 'possessions', and hung with European ownership titles: British India, Dutch East Indies, French Indo-China, German East Africa and so on. Trade routes opened up by these owners carried everything from silk and spices to human flesh westward. All this went on for several hundred years and it was real enough. But the proposition that this scenario was based on was probably the most ingenious and imaginative fiction we have ever heard, mythologizing Europe as the centre of the world, inhabiting it with a superior race and bestowing upon it a monopoly of civilization, all of which then gave it the right to conquer and make use of non-Europe for its profit and pleasure. Non-Europe in this scenario was a mixed bag of 'lesser breeds' – a wonderfully expressive phrase immortalized by the imperial poet, Kipling – and these 'lesser breeds' were long overdue for European enlightenment.

These flights of fantasy would have faded like the fantasies they were, if they had not yielded so much profit, and had not therefore been glued and hammered into place with blood and iron and legitimized by a massive scaffolding of words and images and pseudo-scientific theories in their support. Generations grew up and died, doomed to inferiority, believing there was no way out of this scenario which posed as a true and natural state of affairs. And outdated and hackneyed though this situation now sounds, it is so very recent that South Africa struggled out of its stranglehold only a few years ago.

What difference can this or any other outer casing make to our lives? Does the lie that others impose on us as history affect ordinary people's ongoing lives? Does it affect the aromas of your grandmother's cooking or the sound of rain on your roof or your love for your beloved? And aren't these basically what the human process is all about? Yet it is this outer casing that becomes the framework we are compelled to act within and travel through, burdened with itineraries that may or may not be of our own choosing, but that nevertheless dominate our journey and colour our mentality. And history does dog our footsteps, even and especially for those of us who have left our soil of origin and acquired new nationalities. When has the kind of world we lived in not moved into us, even though we might not even be aware of its major events and upheavals? The mentality that flourished in a flat world was quite different from the grander one that dawned on a globe whose seas men could navigate, and still grander is it now that we live in a boundless cosmos holding worlds upon worlds still waiting to be discovered. Our outer casing affects us powerfully, and we are squaring our account with it in big and intimate ways every day of our lives. In fact, in our own era, the line between public and private has been a continually disappearing one, as vast numbers of people have had to face the traumatic consequences of public events in their private lives. The gap between public and private is in any case infinitesimal in all societies that are in transition. When politics enters daily life, those who write, among others, are forced to take sides, and it becomes impossible to separate politics from literature or any other department of life. In such an environment, literature would be floating in a void if it did not enter the arena.

When great areas of the world were released from the cast-iron outer casing of empire, the horizon was revealed, the skies expanded and we came out of our silences. The first thing this set us free to do was to speak, from points of view based on assumptions and findings that had had no hearing till then. We had something of value to contribute: a point of view, another way of looking at the world, an alternative art of politics, of love and marriage, of medicine, philosophy and nutrition. We believed these alternative approaches might even lead to some useful shifts in perspective, and would find their due place in the mainstream of affairs which until then had been undilutedly Western. But at this moment another scenario invented elsewhere was launched on us. The bombs dropped on Hiroshima and Nagasaki had let loose a reign of terror in the shape of an escalating arms race that kept the world on the brink of a third world war as the two superpowers matched weapon for weapon and fought out their rivalries in proxy wars all over the map. One of them made a hell on earth for ten years in Vietnam and one of their proxy wars has reduced Afghanistan to ruin and destitution. The illusion on which all this devastation and destruction was founded was that two ideologies could not coexist. It had to be either-or.

For those of us who did not see life in these black-and-white categories or see peace in terms of an armed race and armed camps, it was all rather bewildering. The armed camp called the Free World, which the non-aligned were being persuaded to join, looked like a cocktail of dictatorships and theocracies besides democracies. But apart from this, taking sides made no sense to those who did not *want* to restrict themselves to the *either* or the *or* on offer. We felt kindly towards both, and though each camp warned us of the evils of the other, we hobnobbed with both the capitalists and the communists and felt both were necessary for a world in need of more than one solution. In India, we had a hoary tradition of communal living and common ownership of land and individual enterprise. We had no intention of becoming a trophy of either camp by joining its military alliances. But like it or not, and even if one rejected the straitjacket of either-or, everyone had to revolve around the remarkable fiction that the human race is too tiny to accommodate two ideas.

Khruschev once told a joke against himself at a dinner party at the Indian embassy in Moscow. He said he had been touring the country and had come across an ancient ragged peasant. He thumped him on the back and asked him, 'Well, grandfather, and how has life been treating you since the Great October Revolution?' The ancient one said miserably, 'Look at me, comrade. Before the Great October Revolution I had two coats to wear. Since the revolution I've had only this one, and it is so tattered it is falling off my back.' Khruschev said heartily, 'Count your blessings, grandfather. Do you know there are countries in the world where people are running around naked because they have absolutely nothing to wear?' The peasant gave a gloomy nod and said, 'In that case, comrade, they must have had *their* Great October Revolution long before ours.'

I wasn't there on the occasion but I have wondered why on earth Khruschev didn't come to the adult conclusion that it was time to compromise and give the Great October Revolution a hefty dose of rugged individualism. He might have saved his country from collapse, as America would have saved itself decades of paranoia if it had admitted there was another view of world affairs besides its own.

A scene from Satyajit Ray's film *Pratidwandi* illustrates the point of view many of us were in sympathy with at the time. In the film the hero appears for a job interview. The interviewer asks him what, in his opinion, is man's greatest modern achievement. He replies that it is the heroism of the Vietnamese. As this is the time when Neil Armstrong has just landed on the moon, one of the interviewers asks him why he has placed Vietnamese valour above the moon landing, and he says the moon landing is a triumph of technology, while Vietnam is a triumph of the human spirit.

The either-or hysteria came to an end when the Soviets opened up their system. With glasnost and perestroika it collapsed of its own weaknesses, and the Soviet Union disintegrated under its new pressures. But no sooner had this happened than we were ushered into yet another version of reality that many of us were having a hard time subscribing to, which was that unrestrained competition held the key to the kingdom of heaven, and the Lord had proven this by vanquishing communism. This latest figment of imagination from elsewhere is being fitted into place by a process known as the globalization of markets, and the market mantra is now the law. It is now the outer casing, the current interpretation of history that we are having to live within.

There is nothing wrong with globalization. Who doesn't want to be part of a changing world, and reap the benefits thereof? But which world? Is it going to be one we can still recognize ourselves in, and have had some little share in designing? As things stand, we are not even sure of a welcome in some parts of it. In spite of all we hear about boundaries dissolving, never did boundaries look solider than they do now, with immigration barriers rising higher and racism taking to the streets. The perils of passage through those barriers, and once through them, the perils of arrival, are not so far items that the globalizers have included on their agenda. Maybe that is yet to come, but so far the agenda is not startlingly new. In a manner of speaking, colonization was a form of globalization. It built roads and railways, opened sea routes and extended communications to connect up the empire and speed up commerce. Today it is not a one-way process. The globalizers of markets have to consult national sovereignties and seek permissions. Some of their former possessions have become economies to reckon with. There is discussion and bargaining in international forums. But it revolves around the ground rules laid down by the financial institutions of the West, and it is they who carry the day. And industrial interests are so heavily backed by their governments that aid can be withdrawn and sanctions imposed when markets cannot be had for the asking; and when access to a vital commodity such as oil looks threatened, governments think nothing of going to war, as they did in the Gulf.

Within this compulsory marketization of the world, which a friend of mine calls market terrorism, our colonized minds are still hung over with older inflictions. Concepts like modernization and development have automatically been taken to mean what the West understands by them. Levels of industry and technology are judged by Western standards. Non-Europe, without its own criteria, has no option but to struggle on in imitation of the models and standards set up in the West. This has its own fallout in poor societies. But apparently this is a race that now has to be run, and in circumstances where essential power, from finance to information and armaments, is largely controlled by the West. The nuclear club, with its one non-Western member, is a particularly terrifying monopoly. How it can demand a ban on the proliferation of nuclear weapons when it refuses to disarm itself is hard to understand, since the only way to prevent the spread of weapons is by universal disarmament. And why nuclear arsenals should be considered safe in the hands of these club members – one of whom is the only country to have put these bombs to actual use – is another bit of reasoning that is hard to fathom. Old sins have long shadows, and the shadows of the bombs dropped on Hiroshima and Nagasaki still lie over us, with the race for nuclear arms continuing, and armaments a thriving industry without whose sales the prosperous economies would be much less prosperous. The world is not a cosy place at this point in time. Who can rest easy in such a world?

And who can rest assured that the redrawing of maps has made it a world where all human beings have equal status? A few months ago, on the fiftieth anniversary of the end of the Second World War, I watched programmes about the Holocaust. There was also an official apology from Germany for this crime. I was curious about what slant and coverage would be given to the anniversary of Hiroshima. It was mentioned in the news, of course, but the horrific aspect of the atomic bombs was ignored. Though Japan had expressed remorse for its aggression and its wartime oppression of Asian nations, no international leader was present at the ceremony at the memorial, and only a junior United Nations official. And far from there being an apology from the United States for the worst genocide of all time, there were justifications of the event, and a celebration of a golden anniversary, the fiftieth birthday of the atom bomb. Apparently no one need apologize for exterminating the 'lesser breeds'. You will forgive me if I can't think of this world as globalized. And if you ask me what all this has to do with an ACLALS conference, and the field of literature, I would have to say, what else is consciousness composed of but the age it lives in, and if writers do not in some way reflect that age, what are they writing about?

The aim of globalization seems to be the creation of a monoculture, so that every place on earth will end up looking like Kansas City. The metaphor of Kansas City occurred to me because of the song in the musical, *Oklahoma,* which goes: 'Everything's up-to-date in Kansas City, they've gone about as far as they can go.' But this is that brand of packaged programmed change that makes short work of history and continuity, and if you have a lot of those, you have a lot to lose. Once the varieties of human culture have been transformed into varieties of tourism, what need is there for memory? That is the process we, in my part of the world, seem to be caught in, and never did an outer casing make such zombies of us, take hold of body, brain and entrails as fast as this one shows every sign of doing. Globalization of this sort looks like one more form of fundamentalism because it sees itself as the one and only way ahead, the only path to progress, when we know very well that nothing of the sort can be true. The oldest wisdom is that there is no single wisdom. Take the matter of diet. The experts keep coming to us with different rules but no one has yet said the last word on what's good for us. Every other day the last word changes. There's a story about a diet researcher who went to interview a ninety-year-old man and asked him how he accounted for his longevity. The ninety-year-old raised a trembling finger and said, 'No drop of liquor ever touched my lips.' The researcher wrote this down and then asked how the old gentleman could put up with all the noise coming from upstairs, the singing and dancing and yelling, and the ninety-year-old shrugged, 'Oh, that's just Dad, drunk as usual.'

It seems to me that I've always lived in a world according to elsewhere. The concepts it was based on, the point of view it held, were taught to me in textbooks, not as the West's contribution to knowledge, but as indisputable knowledge, and canonized as truths. These were not only the political scenarios written elsewhere. There have been all kinds of scenarios, resting on all kinds of assumptions, that had no particular validity for us, but which all too often we did not challenge or question, not just because they came from that fashionable, powerful and influential elsewhere, but because there seemed no exit from it, no other intellectual space to move in. Let's take the example of psychology, since Freud and Jung and psychoanalysis have dominated life and literature in this century. Why should we be blown before them like leaves in a wind? *Are* Greek myths and Oedipus and other complexes really pivotal to our understanding of our sexual natures? Are there perhaps other ways of exploring states of consciousness? Why not let those in elsewhere sort out their problems with their sons and lovers on psychiatrists' couches or spill their guts out on television talk shows? What reason is there to be trapped in an alien point of view? And if this is an age known as postmodern, then wouldn't postmodern, like modern, perhaps have a different meaning and implications for us than these concepts have in elsewhere, where they originated? Concepts travel, and travel changes them. Feminism is a case in point. Though autonomy is the goal of women's struggles for equality everywhere, issues of sheer survival and basic human needs give ours a more tormenting dimension.

Again, what is so final or inevitable or attractive for *us* about the economic system that Western postmodernism has laid down, complete with its structure, its goals and its values? Do we really go along with an ideology of no-holds-barred competition and aggressive individualism in which family, community, the contacts and responsibilities between generations, the welfare of the weak and vulnerable play no part? Is it really possible that man is an endless consumer whose happiness lies in endless consumption; that more and more toys must be produced for him to play with; that in effect he's no better than a grunting pig with gargantuan appetites, and stuffing those appetites is the right and proper way for him to live? These theories are not alien only to non-Europe. The idea that life is nourished on greed-and-grab and there is no moral law beyond material satisfactions must be repugnant to every society on earth. How and why such notions have found gurus and disciples I cannot say – though these *are* times when all manner of bizarre cults find huge followings – but obviously this particular cult has to be knocked out of existence, laughed out of court, so that if history has indeed come to a stop, as an American academic would have us believe, we can get it going again without delay, and human beings can resume their march to a more civilized level of living, and out of the pigs' trough they have been shoved into by the new economic philosophers.

Quite apart from history being allowed to go on, it would be nice if literature went on too. Will it? I wonder if those who write will be able to disassociate themselves from any outer wrappings they find uncomfortable so that they can feel free to transmit their own individual perceptions. Empires, after all, were unmade not merely by new arrangements of words on a page, but the new visions and intensities felt through them. Black immigrant literatures have hacked life and laughter and lyricism out of the unrelenting societies around them by exercising their own independent imaginations and not the ghosts of others. But these achievements took for granted the preservation of an inner freedom in the absence of external freedom. Great works have come out of unfree conditions, as in nineteenth century Russia, the Soviet Union, East Europe or Latin America. Whether it can happen in India, in the future that is now upon us, I don't know. I don't live in a metropolitan centre and I try *not* to keep up with trends, but the impression I have is that the Indian elite are entranced with the excitement of eating a potato chip made with French collaboration and buying a Maidenform bra. I should explain that until recently India had severely restricted imports in order to build up her own industrial infrastructure, so the flood of foreign goods is a novelty. To judge by the glittering goods advertised, and their skyrocketing prices, or by the magazine articles and TV programmes about the rich and famous, whose celebrity rests on how many times a year they pop over to Paris or New York, one could easily come to the conclusion that we are a jet-propelled society, living in a limbo of limitless luxury, and that there's no such place as India any more.

Instead of the crackle of ideas there once was, inanity rules the day. Newspapers are remaking themselves to become more marketable, and since markets don't need editors, this disappearing breed has gone into other media jobs and been replaced by marketing managers. Publishers, like some of their counterparts elsewhere, have become purveyors of merchandise. And the electronic media, which now has a unique opportunity to use the latest technology to project the themes and images that concern us, is giving impeccable imitations of tasteless fare from the West. The pornography hitting the market follows suit, and this is truly disappointing as one had expected something more original than the regulation nude centrefolds, and what the textile tycoon's ex-mistress told her rival after their fourth double scotch on the rocks. From the inheritors of Kama Sutra, Khajuraho and other sophisticated splendours in word and stone, one had hoped for a touch of class. But just as McDonald's rubbery hamburger may soon drive the sublime shami kebab out of the market, our pornographers have settled for dreary derivative porn instead of blazing a new trail. As we were once interpreted by others through the lenses of the Raj, we are now interpreting ourselves in the jargon, and by the norms and market values, of globalization. As a child I was once shown the newspaper picture of Mahatma Gandhi striding up the stairs of Buckingham Palace in his loincloth, for a meeting with His Majesty the King. Looking back, there is a magnificence about that picture. It seems to symbolize how two cultures *should* meet, each with its dignity and integrity intact.

The Indian scene is much more Indian than the zombie-like rush for buying, selling and mimicking, hallowed by the media and the advertisers. Our virtues and our vices are all our own. Politics, once an altar for self-sacrifice and idealism, now offers dazzling criminal opportunities. The classic villains of fiction and cinema in the 1930s and '40s – the landlords, the moneylenders, the priests – begin to look like babes in arms compared with the dashing new breed. Then we've got militant Hinduism, two words which since time began could never be linked because they were mutually contradictory. Now efforts are being made to join them by politicians who are busy rewriting Indian history, and to listen to the chit-chat on the lawns and in the bars of exclusive clubs, about 800 years of Hindu–Muslim culture might never have existed. There have been changes at every level, the major ones being convulsions in the caste structure that have stood the caste system on its head. The once backward castes govern states and control positions of wealth and power. The Western-educated high-caste elite to whom the British transferred power in 1947 have long since had their day. The several hundred million Indians blotted out by the advertisers are demonstrating their clout in ways we like and don't like. Will the writers among us have a sense of the history that has brought all this about? Will they say anything of all this? Will we carry the awareness that will translate into what we alone have to offer, and not just into cleverness and special effects?

The best writers in the West have their national and group experiences branded into them – their French and Russian and American revolutions, their golden ages and disasters. We were branded, by training in their histories and literatures and methodologies, more with their experiences than our own. But this was a condition that was passing when the current known as globalization swept us on the road to Kansas City and swept everything from sausages to writing into the same market-value production line. Gobbled into this new framework from elsewhere, what can a pen put on paper but words that have no past, and probably very little future? There may well be words that will attract investment in the industry that writing has become; words that may take us backward, concocting versions of the orient as it is still expected to be, complete with ethnic flourishes and misty mysticisms and bags of tricks. The Indian writer, Mulk Raj Anand, points out the contrast in angle of vision between his own story of an orphan in his novel *Coolie*, who is a real Indian orphan, and Kipling's colourful fantasy character, Kim, who helps the British to protect their Indian empire from the Russians. Will we be back to variations of *Kim*? Or will we be seduced by the mechanized, globalized words and images spawned by the new technologies and divorced from our own context and conditions? For people whose main resource is their imagination, technology may reserve its most death-dealing devices. I know technology is sacrosanct and has been written into the scripture of what is known as progress, but there must be a point beyond which we do not let it usurp our human functions, and that point may well have been reached. But mesmerized by it, will we in India well and truly return to being creatures of elsewhere?

I am reminded of a friend of mine years ago in Bombay, a cultivated, elegant, much admired woman. There was something about her that used to puzzle me, that I couldn't quite place, until I realized that if I closed my eyes and shut out her dark skin and her sari, and thought of her as an upper class Englishwoman, everything about her fell into place. In India the old order died no violent death. It was bowed out. In the drawing rooms of Bombay high society in the late 1950s, it was still very much around. My friend charmingly reflected its accent, its conversation, its culture. These were the masks Indians had once worn in order to be invited to the ball as it were, to be acceptable in ruling circles, and a good many of them had never taken them off. Maybe they had become a second skin and they felt more comfortable with them than with the Indian reality around them, or maybe their indoctrination had made them incapable of a relationship with India, except as outsiders, and unfit for any role except one in a masquerade. I told her once that I had been to the airport to receive Ho Chi Minh and found him one of the gentlest and most affectionate of men, and this filled her with genuine amazement, for she genuinely believed he was a monster. She also believed India was not going to last out the next decade. The country was going to fall apart. A foreign think tank had told her so. Thus, when we wear masks, do the demons of others become our demons, and their gods, our gods? And I have an overwhelming sense of deja vu today as I look around me when I go to Delhi, which is more advanced in matters of globalization than Dehra Dun, where I live. It seems to me we are yet again acting and reacting within the confines of a provided framework. Perhaps it is still a case of having to wear a mask or not being invited to the ball. It is certainly still the case that the journeys we make continue to take us westward, to what is still the centre of the world.

It is these journeys to what is still the centre of the world, a Mecca even in our own consciousness, that create the illusion that, because varieties of people flock to that Mecca, we are now living in a cosmopolitan era; that literature too is becoming cosmopolitan, unfettered by frontiers or a frontier consciousness, and that it no longer needs to start from a place of its own. This bit of logic is like the Miss Universe contest, which chooses the most beautiful woman in the universe from twenty-one glamourous contestants, after which she goes on to advertise Coca Cola. The word cosmopolitan similarly covers a handful compared with the mass of people who feel at home only in a particular soil, many of them untouched by outer trends. 'Cosmopolitan' has about it the exclusive luxurious tinkle of privileged culture. When I hear that the world is fast becoming cosmopolitan, or that it is now a global village, I feel I must be living in another world, not the one all the experts are talking about. And I think this is entirely possible since it is far from being One World.

Speaking at an ACLALS conference a few years ago I asked when post-colonial would stop being post-colonial. Now I wonder when exile stops being exile. I'm not sure I understand the word the way it is now used, to cover so many variations on the theme. I have come across book reviews referring to the book's author as exiled. Recently I came across a book which was partly about the effects of exile on writers and their writing. The dictionary definition, which is banishment, or long absence from one's country, would not fit them all. Can exile, when it is the result of choosing to live somewhere else, be exile? Can such a person's state of mind and being, however nostalgic, in any way resemble the sense of displacement and loss that plagues those who have been forced to leave home, as political or economic refugees? Can the label of exile be pinned on all expatriate writing? I read very little criticism, and I know nothing about its vocabulary, so I may he quite wrong in thinking that the word exile has acquired a cult flavour, and come to have extravagant all-purpose meanings, almost as if Rupert Murdoch, on acquiring American nationality, had become an exile.

In 1992, the *Guardian* published a series of articles under the heading 'Writing Home', in which writers around the world reflected on their nationality, and described their feelings for the country they called home. I thought I would find in these articles a rejection of the sentiment people once attached to their native soil, even a thankfulness at having shed all that, either metaphorically, or by literally moving to new territory. I thought my own contribution to the series would show up an unfashionable attachment to my roots in an age when cross-cultural connections are supposed to matter more than roots. I thought I would be in a minority of one. To my surprise there were several like me, for whom a national identity was not only *not* out of date, but a source of selfhood. Two of these writers, with opportunities to settle in the West, decided to remain in their authoritarian homelands. The Chinese writer, Zhang Xianliang, had spent twenty-two years in a labour camp and was still not being published in China, yet these are his words:

> Perhaps there are some who belong to the world and not to one country. I cannot be such a person. In my body and spirit I can belong only to China. I do not believe that there can be a truly universal literature which is not attached to any particular society. Even Shakespeare's works belong in the end to England.

The Czech writer, Ivan Klima, was visiting London when Soviet troops invaded Czechoslovakia, but he went home. In his words:

> ... home, where at any moment the police could ring the doorbell and search my flat, take me off for interrogation or even arrest me. Home where my wife was continually getting the sack, where I didn't know whether my children would be allowed to study, and where I was banned from publishing .... But I was born here and have accepted it as destiny that my home is here. The worst thing for me would be to discover that my home is nowhere, or that it is everywhere, which is no more than a substitute for ... 'nowhere,' and is intended to fill more easily that empty space in the soul which the loss of home tends to leave behind.

Likewise, Shusako Endo of Japan, who writes about the suffering of the Japanese during the war, the horror of the atomic strikes, the humiliation of defeat, and what Japan has lost in the race to become an industrialized power, concludes: 'However, as a Japanese, I cannot desert Japan.' And Chinua Achebe of Nigeria, who had no choice but to leave Nigeria if he wanted to stay alive, writes: 'The hard words Nigeria and I have said to each other look like words of anxious love, not hate.' Shusako Endo also writes: 'Many Japanese – especially the young – are gripped by a sense of emptiness. One manifestation of this is the ... large number of people travelling overseas.' It would seem that the plant of universalism, at least according to these writers, is itself a product of having stayed rooted. And incidentally, I've often wondered what sort of books Henry James would have written if *he'd* stayed home during the wonderful turbulent years of America's tremendous growth as a nation.

True cosmopolitanism, which would mean partaking of a world culture, cannot exist, there being no world culture, only the Europe-centredness that substitutes for one. On the other hand, wars of identity rage all about us, including here on this once serene island, and few are as fortunate as Naipaul in being able to sort out their enigmas of identity in peaceful, affluent surroundings. Those countries of Europe that are the most advanced and stable areas of the world are just as fiercely obsessed with their identity, and with keeping their racial identity unsullied, when they pass laws to restrain or prohibit non-white immigration. Whether identity bares its teeth and claws in actual battle, or dresses soberly and speaks in suave accents, or is simply the need within us to stay home, it is very much with us.

But if all I have said sounds like a plea for nationalism, my plea is for the very opposite. Separateness is probably the most absurd and dangerous of all illusions. There never was a time when it was a sound idea. My own belief is in a reconciliation of cultures, of the sort that Nelson Mandela and Aung San Su Kyi have come to represent in politics. It is not time for me to become more like you, and to pattern myself on your ways, or to write what pleases you. What it is time for is for us to harmonize our ways of living and thinking, so that we will never be strangers to one another again, so that from a relationship that partakes of all our identities, a truly cosmopolitan world, and a genuinely universal literature, can arise.

An Aspect of Terror*

In a novel I wrote in 1972 called *The Day in Shadow*, a young divorced woman who is in difficulties over her crippling divorce settlement and her life ahead, is having tea with an elderly friend, Ram Krishan, and this bit of dialogue takes place.

> 'Yes,' she said, 'I have wondered about that often. I have wished non-violence had become a way of thinking, made into a law, or given some kind of sanction, so that it could be passed on like an inheritance. I've wanted to pass it on to my son. Until one can, it's no use .... So that's why I have nothing to give my children, because I have nothing to give them except non-violence.'
>
> Her laugh had a tremble to it. She went on talking nervously.
>
> 'I mean, how do you give them non-violence in an attractive package, something they can be sure will work in the world around them, unless they see it working first?'
>
> My dear, Ram Krishan wanted to say, my dear, don't be despairing. There is a world like that very near us, around the corner if you look for the signs. You in your lifetime may reach out and touch it, if you have the courage and the endurance, if you believe.

---

* Plenary Address at Conference on 'Terror: Its Representations and Politics', 9 April 1995, University of Kent, Canterbury

How absurdly irrelevant those words sound in an age that is probably more viciously violent, worldwide, than any age past. Twelve years after I wrote them, my cousin, who was then prime minister, was gunned to death by religious fanatics. Seven years later her son was shredded to pulp in a bomb blast by an ethnic fundamentalist. Yet in such times especially, what other remedy is there but non-violence? It is in any case the path of evolution, and the way the world will be in time to come. But meanwhile there are ordeals by fire to be gone through, some of long standing, and I want to talk about one of them which goes relentlessly on.

Most people do not belong to the European fold, to what still operates as the world's mainstream culture, but they live perforce in a world which is still dominated, in all vital particulars, by the West. This makes for a perverse situation, assigning the larger part of humanity to the position of a beleaguered minority. Psychologically, this imposes a perpetual sense of isolation and otherness, and in practical affairs it continues to ignore or marginalize the many, leaving them little or no say in how the world is run, however damaging the course it takes may be to their lives, their health and their interests. Those outside the privileged and well-guarded frontiers of the mainstream have to put up not only with the routine humiliations thrust on them by racial arrogance, but also with the aggressive forms that arrogance takes in trade, defence, immigration and other policies, and even in methods of warfare and peacemaking. The dividing line between Europe, i.e., the West, and non-Europe seems designed to separate the human from subhuman species. It is specifically this, and not only the aggression and injustices involved, that I am calling an aspect of terror.

When a state of affairs has been as long established as Western supremacy has been, it comes to be considered normal. The ancient world had slaves and free men. Jefferson's America declared all men equal, and no paradox was perceived in the fact that he, and perhaps other signatories to the declaration, owned hundreds of slaves. And almost up to the present time the world was divided into the ruling and the subject races. The long shadow of Europe, as concept and culture, loomed large, as of right, over human affairs, and the felt reality of being human, and of what constituted a human being, was a privilege claimed by that race and culture alone. Western dominance was not just the reigning political reality which one challenged, if at all, at one's own peril. It was enshrined as the normal, rational, and only possible state of affairs. Even those who opposed it found it hard to visualize any other kind of world order. Domestic relations came under somewhat the same dispensation when the physical and financial ownership of the wife by the husband was taken for granted. There are no circumstances so hard to dislodge, in public or private life, as those that look like a normal respectable condition.

Things have, of course, changed. No absolute dividing line now separates the rulers from the ruled. Some of the so-called subject races have crossed poverty lines and moved closer to Western standards and lifestyles. Some have become factors to reckon with, and the one-time rulers now include them. The rulers too cannot be lumped together. They do not behave alike, nor do they represent a single monolithic point of view. There is probably no parallel to the voluntary withdrawal of the British from India, and few relationships between ruler and ruled have done as well as this one, including the efforts Britain is making to integrate her now multiracial population. But by and large, equality and control over one's fate remain out of the reach of most, in a global arrangement where the West continues to occupy a vast political space by virtue of the fact that it controls the institutions of power: trade and industry, finance, information and armaments, and the technology that serves all these; and uses these levers as it sees fit, including war as a tool of policy, when a crucial commodity is involved, as in the Gulf War.

All this has been true in time past. Blood and commerce have gone together. It is what the violent history of imperialism was all about. But empires did not pretend otherwise, and they did not have the huge apparatus of modern technology at their disposal. Nor was economic adventure in the past able to bank on a philosophy of unbridled and undiluted consumerism as its rationale, or on greed as a desirable way of life. Now there are no ideological or moral restraints on the process. Wiped clean of debate or doubt, unimpeded by the more civilized aspects of a twentieth-century conscience, commercial interests that are thousands of miles distant from the markets they target on the map, not only decide on the pressures to be used – sanctions, withdrawal of aid and loans, military strikes – but they also do so by judging other societies, and the value of a human life in them, much as they did in the days of slavery and empire, by where they happen to be located on the map. And if this judgement then translates into international trade policies that are indifferent to the survival, livelihood, stability or self-respect of millions of people, so be it, since people who are not recognized as fellow human beings cannot be sinned against.

The jungle that goes by the name of commerce in any case knows no sin, but even the laws of the jungle have not been observed in double standards of industrial safety which have suddenly come to light when death-dealing disasters have taken place, like the gas explosion at the Union Carbide plant in Bhopal, India, which classically demonstrates the expendability of the poor. The compensation for a life lost has been about $1,860 and to the injured about $540. Ten years after the event, those who are working for the welfare of its victims report an increase in respiratory disorders, cataracts, spontaneous abortions, TB and cancer cases.

It is also well known that pharmaceutical firms sell drugs in the Third World that are banned as dangerous by their own governments. And selective anti-environment and anti-human policies have been directly responsible for dislocation and impoverishment on a mass scale. On global warming, for which we are told the rich countries that over-consume the earth's natural resources are overwhelmingly responsible one of the new economic philosophers has advised that nothing much need be done about it since the high-income countries can profitably adapt to it and in a hundred years its impact on them will be negligible. In his words, 'The winners will be happy, the losers will be miserable.' According to a scientific forecast, these losers are expected to die in tens of millions by the mid-twenty-first century, but the economic advice to wait and see suits the multinational oil and coal industries, and we live in times when science plays second fiddle to profits. What will amount to a ferocious form of ethnic cleansing is permissible if it profits industry, and if those who are killed qualify racially as sacrificial victims. A similar 'economic logic' justifies the dumping of toxic waste on African countries, which logic the former chief economist of the World Bank has called 'impeccable'. The powerless can expect no mercy, but if you happen to be a successful Asian competitor in any area of the market, you will find yourself up against measures unrelated to trade, to prevent your becoming a threat to industries in the West that cannot face competition.

The double standard governing intellectual property rights has an unmatched irony of its own. China's pirating of American software and other items has been much in the news. Reverse piracy and plunder are never heard about on the information networks that rule the skies. It's an idea I put into my novel *Mistaken Identity:* Comrade Dey is in jail in 1929 on the charge of a conspiracy to overthrow the King Emperor. He remarks to one of his fellow prisoners, 'Capitalists have a weird sense of proportion. Hours can be spent in their courts of law attacking and defending a man who has purloined a penknife. But sail out and loot a country, bash up the population and make a scavengers' feast of their remains, and you go down in history as Something the Great.'

But such is the chronic imbalance, and ingrained terrorism, of a mentality that holds whole populations in contempt and treats their countries as raw material to be recklessly exploited, at no matter what cost to human beings and by financial intimidation or military intervention if need be, so that otherwise unsustainable standards of extravagance and opulence and wasteful spending may be enjoyed by the world's most prosperous people – and then only by the prosperous among them.

We can defend Salman Rushdie and Taslima Nasreen against government-sanctioned or government-permitted terrorism, but defence against savage or unprincipled international behaviour in the name of trade not only escapes the terrorist label, it is now dignified by the label of globalization of markets. As the terms and conditions of globalization are laid down by the West, it is, as ever, the Western agenda, and not a broader human agenda, that is being pursued. It is one that defines modern as Western and assumes that all societies want to look, live and think like Europeans or North Americans. And many of the well off in non-European societies are so indoctrinated by this assumption that they become enthusiastic collaborators and willing accomplices in a brand of fundamentalism which is as fanatic – because it is as non-negotiable – as the religious or ethnic variety. For those who are at the sacrificial end of globalization, it is not a new global era of mutual benefit and profit. For them, it's more like ongoing history – history as exclusion, as rejection and as apartheid.

Until I became an adult, there was no such thing as human rights for any black person on earth. They were a monopoly of the West. It was difficult enough for others to be considered human, much less a human being with rights. In these circumstances it is extraordinary that the West makes human rights an article of foreign or trade policy, withholding or granting favours on the basis of a country's human rights record, when human rights are precisely what they have slaughtered for centuries, and which are under ruthless attack by Western fundamentalism today in the policies which the powerful pursue against the powerless. America's sudden humanitarianism, and her current hard line on this issue, is particularly puzzling in the light of her own dismal record of staunch support – even with lethal armaments to guarantee their survival – of one dictatorship after another. Democracy itself, not long ago, was dismissed as a utopian and unreliable idea for developing countries. Much better the military gang you could do business with and remote-control.

But the double standard is most shockingly demonstrated by the nuclear debate. Arsenals of nuclear weapons are still maintained by the nuclear powers who know they cannot use them against each other, since such a war would be total and unwinnable. No weapon is for use against an adversary who can match it. One must conclude that they are for use against the unarmed, to be kept in reserve as the ultimate weapon of terror, and used as and when mass genocide is judged necessary. Why else, instead of agreeing to eliminate these altogether, and calling for global disarmament, do the nuclear powers claim it their exclusive and perpetual right to stay nuclear, while they insist that the rest of the world disarm? Any formula that divides the world into nuclear and non-nuclear nations is as unrealizable as it is hypocritical. Without their total ban their spread cannot be stopped, and on what possible basis of moral superiority can their ownership be limited to a chosen few? The country now leading the campaign to prevent proliferation, and the dangers attending it, is the only country ever to have acted so dangerously as to use this weapon; and whose record in war besides includes more explosives dropped on the peasants of Indo-China than had been manufactured up to that time in history. A basic human right – the right to live without fear – is violated when such weapons exist in any hands at all.

The present freeze on fissile materials that America is now proposing was, in fact, originally proposed by the group of eight non-aligned countries at the United Nations as long ago as 1966, along with a comprehensive test ban, a gradual reduction of the stock of weapons, a ban on the use of nuclear weapons and an assurance of security for non-nuclear states. None of this was acceptable at the time because it was part of the West's weapons Bible to match weapon for weapon against other nuclear adversaries. The present partial change in attitude comes about because, according to defence analysts, the United States (and very likely, the other nuclear powers) have an abundance of fissile material and can afford a freeze on it. This would also make the American insistence on non-proliferation sound more plausible. Yet in this discriminatory context the Nuclear Non-Proliferation Treaty – as a substitute for global disarmament – sounds exactly like the Nazis making the Jews wear the Star of David, the easier to identify them for come what may.

I was wondering, as I watched the fiftieth anniversary commemoration of the Auschwitz holocaust on TV earlier this year, what kind and amount of coverage the media would give to the fiftieth anniversary of Hiroshima and Nagasaki in August – when in hardly a second some 150,000 people were vapourized or burned to cinders, and some 100,000 subsequently died agonizing deaths from the effects of radiation. Fortunately, the US postal department seems to have abandoned its plan to issue postage stamps showing the destruction of the two cities with the caption that the atom bombs shortened the war. I don't know what kind of exhibition the Smithsonian Institution in Washington is putting on to commemorate the event, but Mr Newt Gingrich has been reported as saying that ex-servicemen need have no fear it will make Americans proud.

The point I am making is that millions have not yet been accorded full human status. The Japanese in 1945 were not just the enemy. In a war where the mass slaughter of civilian populations was commonplace, they were singled out for apocalyptic punishment. It troubled no Western conscience that they, being regarded as subhuman, could be made use of as guinea pigs in an atomic experiment. Somewhat similarly, at the end of the Gulf War, American journalists hailed it as having been miraculously almost casualty-free. 'No people were killed in this war,' was their opinion. Apart from tens of thousands of troops pulverized in their trenches in forty-three days of air war, there is no count of the massacres in residential areas, schools, hospitals and places of worship, or the famous bombing of the air raid shelter. But the talk-show journalists were right. No people were killed. These were not people. By the same token, sanctions can continue against Iraq (largely at America's insistence) to starve a population into submission.

It is the horror at the heart of every genre of terrorism that it fails to recognize the other, whoever the other may be, as human. But an old and relentless refusal to do so creates the ongoing aspect of terror I have talked about today.

One kind of fundamentalism generates another. The CIA's murder of Mossadeq, who challenged the writ of the oil giants in Iran, eventually gave rise to Ayatollah Khomeini. And this is a theme with historical variations over parts of the world. Societies strike back at what they see as recolonization. In the process they destroy their own modern legacy along with what they target as westernization. So far as my own theme is concerned, perhaps the answer lies in an end to hegemonic ambition, whether political, cultural or economic, and the recognition of others as equals. Those who lead nations have to begin thinking along these lines.

The Myth Reincarnated*

On the subject of cartographies, new or old, and how a changing map of the world affects the concept of identity, the first question I have to ask myself is: What does what we call the world mean, and what is its validity for me? Has the prevailing wisdom about it been valid for me in the past? And is it any truer for me in the present?

To begin with, the world was flat and we would have fallen over the edge if we ventured too far. Then it became round. After that, once its shape was settled, its expanding size took over, and one's view of it, and of the forces of good and evil in it, was fashioned according to where one happened to be situated on the globe. What one perceived as civilization, and what as outer darkness, depended on one's location. Then came Europe's maritime age – those 300-odd years of European exploration, conquest, colonization and empire that were the forerunner of the world we now live in – when sea routes were opened by Europe for commercial traffic and the traffic was one-way. Those centuries established a lasting psycho-cartography of their own, positioning Europe and the Atlantic as fount and centre, and all the rest of the vastness of creation as outlying and peripheral, and created for the purpose of serving

* Address at Conference on 'New Cartographies: Commonwealth and Post-Colonial Literature,' St John's College, Oxford, 6 April 1995. Published in *Journal of Commonwealth Literature,* Vol. XXX, No.I, 1995.

and servicing the centre. Areas were labelled Near, Middle or Far, depending on their distance from the centre and were judged by their usefulness to it. And this is how matters still stood when I was a child, growing up in a small town in north India, a town famous for landmarks that had figured in the Ramayana, beside a river that was sacred to mankind's oldest religion, in a countryside that was heir to a view of life unique for the immensity of its vision and the universality of its outlook. And so, of course, the prevailing wisdom not only had no validity for me, it was complete nonsense.

Yet this was the map of the world, and it was presided over by a breed of men who quite soberly assessed themselves as the rightful arbiters of affairs. The reigning reality divided the map into rulers and the lesser breeds they ruled. There was a master race and there were subject races – a term that was actually used by officialdom to define the larger part of humanity. Embedded and implicit in this scheme of things was a master civilization, Hellenic in origin; a master religion called Christianity, which was in fact a severely edited, sanitized, militarized and westernized version of an Asian religion and its scripture; a master philosophy which started with the Greeks, and from which all legitimate philosophical enquiry and scientific investigation must proceed, since progress, both as idea and development, was an achievement of the West. Following from these there was a master view of life, which was material, and an approach to phenomena that separated organic from inorganic matter, and split the human being into mind and body. All this fragmentation, compartmentalization, and irreconcilability, was enthroned as knowledge, and any other view of life was ignorance and monstrous superstition.

This Western knowledge went into textbooks and was taught in schools, not as Western knowledge but as Knowledge. It was the stuff of public policy and pronouncements, and of scientific articles. Fiction and cinema reflected its biases. A hero, by definition, could not be discovered to have one drop of oriental blood – unless that dark drop were found to be Spanish after all. And it was, of course, the standard by which art was judged. Above all it found its way into prayer, commandeering the kingdom of God as its exclusive monopoly.

Not one of its promoters and propagators dreamed that not one of these propositions would survive the redrawing of the world's map and the surfacing of other points of view, because those who had thus arranged the world for their convenience, and laid down the laws by which alone it must be understood, had persuaded themselves not only of the everlastingness of their arrangement, but also of its inherent rightness. They saw it as part of the cosmic order, as natural and permanent as the solar system, and themselves as its God-appointed upholders. As late as 1936, the Dutch governor general of Indonesia (then the Dutch East Indies) made the remark: 'We have ruled here for three hundred years with the whip and the club and we shall still be doing it in another three hundred years.' As late as 1942, Winston Churchill declared he had not become His Majesty's First Minister in order to preside over the liquidation of the British Empire. He saw no such eventuality in sight, simply because any other order of things was quite unthinkable.

And yet, what was this fundamentalist imperial view but wishful thinking? And what could it lead to but more extreme wishful thinking on a more stupendous scale? For once that genie of land grab, that insatiable paranoia for power and glory, was out of the bottle, who could stop it, or tell where it would end? And if one myth had been such a roaring success, why not another? Where else, then, could all that mythmaking lead but to the spawning of a master race within the master race, and a war to outrival all wars, one that was based on the master myth that blue-eyed blonds had been born to conquer and rule the world? A myth, according to the dictionary, is 'a purely fictitious narrative usually involving supernatural persons and embodying popular ideas on natural phenomena'. And what have we had here on earth, under the cloak of recent, and not so recent, history but that?

I was brought up in an atmosphere of revolution, in a family committed to overturning the imperial order; so I grew up, as I said, believing that the reigning cartography and the doctrines enshrined in it had no more reality than the flat world we were going to fall off the edge of in earlier times, but it was in that colossal outer mythology that we were imprisoned, just as my parents and other patriots were locked up in jails for years of their lives. These people had no way of knowing when their ordeal, and the country's, would end, but they profoundly believed it must, because fictions must come to an end. One day, maybe not in their own lifetime, the distorted world would shift into perspective. Until then they would have to go on rejecting the evidence of solidity and permanence around them, and go on refusing to make terms with it, while they worked for the day when they would run their own lives, and speak for themselves from very different premises and assumptions. Looking back I am filled with wonder at the energy and optimism, but above all the sheer feat of imagination this must have taken, with words such as the Dutch governor general's and Winston Churchill's in their ears, and the awe-inspiring structures of what looked like invincible power all around them.

The day did come. The maps that empires had brought into being were redrawn. A host of countries came to be known as themselves and not as Europe's possessions. The West no longer had a monopoly of political significance. But the task of interpreting oneself in the post-war world ran into immediate and unanticipated hurdles. Let me give you a political example as it is an obvious one. It was the political scene in India that had been radically transformed by the transfer of power, so one hoped to be understood, first and foremost, in this context. My mother went as India's ambassador to the United States in 1949, two years after Independence, to find that the world had once more been arbitrarily classified – by which philosopher I don't know – but this time into the first, second and third categories of a new moral order. My mother utterly failed, as did every Indian ambassador after her, to get the United States to understand India's refusal to line up with either of the two new military blocs, or to throw open the country to unbridled economic adventure either by her own or foreign entrepreneurs, preferring to follow a path of her own between capitalism and state socialism. It seemed the only map the United States recognized consisted of the reach and stretch of NATO and its other security alliances. This area with its bewildering array of dictatorships, theocracies and despotisms was for some reason known as the Free World, and anything that was not gung-ho capitalist was communist. We are all caught up in a particular time and place, and act in very different circumstances. India's was not an end-of-war awareness. It was a start-of-freedom awareness. It was the Indian ambassador's brief to convey her country's intention to chart a course of her own choosing, rather than follow the prescriptions of others, but this simple message was impossible to get across to a mentality that took as its starting point the proposition that inside of every human breast there was an American struggling to come out. Other points of view were regarded as treacherous betrayals. Over breakfast at his house one day, Mr John Foster Dulles who was of a missionary frame of mind, gave my mother to understand that he had prayed for guidance on America's stand on the peace treaty with Japan, and he believed it had the Lord's sanction. It was the Indian ambassador's awkward task to tell him that in that case her prime minister was in disagreement with the Lord.

The prime minister made his first visit to America about that time and was invited to dinner by leaders of industry. By way of introducing the company, and making the significance of the occasion clear his host said, 'Mr Nehru, I want you to know there are X trillion dollars represented around this table.' Nehru, who had not come begging for aid or bounty, and had never heard anyone introduced by the size of his bank account, was rendered temporarily speechless. And the failure of communication continued throughout the visit and for decades afterwards.

Interpretation in other areas was as frustrating. It seemed that authentic Indian music, dance or even a lecture had to be put through a trimming process to fit the fancies and attention span of its audience. The written word met somewhat the same fate. If it was not presented in the form of a puzzled outsider looking in, it had in any case to be a picturesque contrast to the Western mainstream, and not a situation-in-itself that merited its own existence. Automatically, much writing fell into this trap of attention-getting – as often it still does – measuring itself against the yardsticks of the West. To awaken awareness in an audience is hardly possible until one is fully self-aware. And I have often asked myself, are we still catering, seeing ourselves through another's mirror, or have we come away at last, to act and not to react? I am not sure of the answer. Perhaps the answer would not matter if it did not affect a whole human canvas apart from writing.

I write novels with political settings. This was not a deliberate choice. Politics was all I had to work with, if I may use the word to signify a childhood filled with the sound and fury, and overflowing with the yearnings, of the national movement for independence, when all issues – from the cloth you wore to the food you ate and the company you kept – were political issues; when personal and political fates were inextricably bound, and political and social history merged with private lives. I could no more distance myself from that inheritance than a shoemaker's child can escape the smell of shoe leather. Why pin a novel to a political event or a political vision or its betrayal? Because it happened to be the outer focal point that stirred my imagination? It had nothing to do with politics as ideology or message, only with the strong and constant awareness I have had since birth of a concept called India. My fiction was about a de-mythologized India whose people were much the same, as virtuous or as rascally, as anyone else. They had wanted to be free, and once free, they wanted to run their own lives. In the course of doing so the golden landscape of freedom decayed, power corrupted, and idealism became a ghost, but one that still haunted the house. None of this was exotic or mystifying. It was not picturesque or ethnic. It did not present a suitably modified version of a quaint colourful land of Eastern intrigue and Western example. It did not rise out of, or boil down to, the proverbial heat and dust seen through the lenses of the Raj or the after-Raj, because inside of me there was an Indian, buried for centuries, struggling to come out, looking and behaving like an ordinary human being. Because we had had no political voice, I found it especially satisfying to express myself politically and to speak a political idiom that was rootedly Indian, yet modern in its twentieth-century legacy. And it is no secret that India is the hub of my own inspirational universe. What I've tried to do is to discover the sort of behaviour politics and religion breed in the newly independent but ancient society we are.

Cartography turned another cartwheel when the disintegration of the Soviet Union brought another set of maps into being, and yet another moral order whose mantra was the market. An American academic told us that with communism collapsed, history was over. Since it had just restarted for some of us this sounded as peculiar as the Free World had, or the flat world before it, or the saga of the survival of the whitest that had once substituted for history. The collapse of communism began to sound odder when democratic elections brought it back to power in several countries – so far as I can recall, in Bulgaria, Lithuania, Mongolia and the former Yugoslav federation of Serbia and Montenegro. Even in Russia the communists won sixty-four seats, just ten less than Yeltsin's party. And to crown the whole paradox, the world's only Hindu kingdom, Nepal, elected a communist government. Not to mention China, or that India till recently had three communist state governments, one of which is heading for two decades in power. However, it seems to be the prevailing assessment that from now on markets will rule the world through a process known as globalization. The fact of advanced communications and floating populations, which either choose, or are driven by necessity, to live elsewhere, does give a superficial legitimacy to this idea. But globalization looks like the latest incarnation of a rugged old myth, in circumstances where essential power, in the shape of finance and industry, armaments and technology, is still controlled by the West, and the laws of the market divide us up as ever – like entry queues at airports – into sheep and goats, a nobility and a proletariat. From its dangerous trade policies that use Third World lands as dumping grounds for their toxic waste, and brook no interference in the capture of markets to racist immigration policies, globalization looks like a master plan to the same old world. It gives us one more demonstration of that fundamentalist attitude which, since Christopher Columbus, has allowed for no alternative view of God or man.

As for identity, which flourished in the crucible of a fight for freedom, and fought back when it was under attack, now a fake connectedness sabotages the need for struggle. A sense of Indianness first took shape in response to British domination, and the British, like other, older encounters, also expanded and enriched Indian identity. But now as we are regimented and supervised into the images laid down by the managers of the global economy, and re-engineered to fit the culture of endless, mindless consumerism, we will be stripped of family, community and tradition and lose touch with the complex network of material, emotional and spiritual interdependence that goes into the making of a truly human society. All that is exceptional in us, by which we would evolve our own modern personality, will face extinction. Beneath the surface likenesses there will remain deep, unexplored subsurfaces with agendas of their own, whole floating worlds beneath the ruling Western agenda. Somewhere in space the dialogue between Mr John Foster Dulles and my mother – as between the missionary and the heathen – will go on at cross purposes. Mr Nehru will forever sit speechless with shock, encircled by American millionaires. And the uniqueness of India's identity will have to wait for another day to dawn.

As it always does, it will. Its reach and spread will not lie within the four corners of an ideology or imperatives conceived in and laid down by the West. It will not be confined to an atomized, undernourished, obsessively individualistic consciousness. Nor will it be ruled by technology, biology, commerce and the like, though all these will be part of it. In a genuinely new era the very assumptions that have been taken for granted till now may have to change. It may be the East's turn to act as catalyst and agent of change in the modern Western sensibility, as the West has been for us in the past. Until the white man puts down his burden, the redrawing of maps alone cannot become the equalizing experience one naively supposed it would be. The world changes only as one's perception of it changes.

Some Thoughts on the Puzzle of Identity*

There is a meditation technique that takes the form of an inquiry. It is called Koham Dhyana, meaning who am I? This is an unravelling process directed inward from familiar labels like one's name, sex and nationality to the meaning of who, and why, one is – the idea being that true awareness is realized only when we shut out external stimuli, from the sights, sounds and smells that bombard us, to the historical and geographical factors that crowd in on us, and only through the discipline of letting go of everything connected with the ego, until we come to the answer which is both deeply personal and universal. But as this ancient technique requires total silence, it may not be appropriate to try it here in place of this lecture. Failing this, there's only the outside world for answers, a poor substitute that has a way of partitioning and pigeonholing us rather than integrating us. One way to avoid being chopped up into bits might be simply to say: I'm a member of the human race and a citizen of the world, and leave it at that. But given the condition of the world the human race inhabits, with its blessings so unequally distributed and so undemocratically controlled, and ruled as it still is, by the perspective and priorities of those in power, this seems too general an answer – there being nothing much in common

* The Ravenscroft Commonwealth Literature Lecture, University of Leeds, 18 February 1993. Published in *Journal of Commonwealth Literature.*

between citizens on one side of the globe and another. And then it is impossible to ignore all the ferocious wars of identity – national, racial, ethnic and religious – going on in this very world. And though this outer scaffolding does not determine all that we are, it is probably a useful place to start. So my own puzzle starts with India, and the fact that it was British India when I was born.

To put that environment into its historical perspective, it was an India which as a pre-industrial economy – till then a wealthy competitor in eighteenth-century markets – had come under the control of a company of foreign merchants. This, followed by foreign political domination, was probably one of the most effective combinations of political power and vested interest that ever reduced a country to penury and a psyche to fracture. Even or perhaps especially, the benefits of empire – its roads, railways and telegraph wires for example – only made plunder of the land more efficient, while the people were only required to pay their rents and dues to their new landlords and keep their place in the feudal order. Unlike earlier landlords – Turks, Mughals and others who came to stay, be Indianized and absorbed into the bloodstream and the social fabric – the British chose to remain foreign and Olympian, supported by an elaborate, if unstated, system of segregation. There was an Indian society and a white society, and no easy coming and going between them. As a child of parents involved in the national movement for independence, I hardly ever saw the English and all I knew about them was that they were nervous of germs, and put something called antimacassar on their drawing room chairs. Also unlike earlier governments at Delhi, this one saw itself as a civilizing mission, so that a challenge to it was not just a traitorous offence, punished by imprisonment, exile or the gallows, it was an offence against the natural order of things, and the moral order of the universe. This then was the empire my parents were up against, paying for their opposition to it with long prison sentences and other forms of harassment, heartbreak and persecution, and one of them with his life.

Did this make snarling fanatics of them, wanting to tear every Englishman limb from limb? Actually, what it all boiled down to – apart from a refusal to tolerate British rule – was a passionate admiration for British qualities of character, lifelong friendships with English people, English governesses for us children and custard pudding for dinner. Such are the intricacies of any encounter that is to any extent human, never mind what history, economics or statistics tell us, or what the rules lay down. The rules, of course, were there. There were railway compartments, park benches and clubs reserved For Europeans Only, and schools that admitted Indians but whose textbooks and curricula had no connection with India. On the silly side of arrogance the myth of British superiority made it obligatory for the English to mispronounce our names. Years later when I watched Paul Scott's *Jewel in the Crown* I was shocked into remembering the atmosphere of crude white arrogance I had known as a child, one that made every nerve scream protest, as one lived out the hurts and humiliations, the furies and frustrations of trying to become merely visible in a Europe-dominated world, in a world where the West was The World, and the rest of humanity a fringe on its edges.

All this was bad enough without the people who couldn't pronounce our names becoming our interpreters and setting themselves up as intermediaries between us and everybody else. With the exception of those whose dedicated scholarship introduced the Sanskrit classics to the West, and others who became intimate with the splendours and problems of the land, the interpreters were usually the Empire's standard-bearers and saw India in its hallowed light, from Kipling's colourful stories to Winston Churchill's powerful prose. And like the textbooks I had at school, this inspired output had nothing much to do with India. Kipling's stories were about Europeans in the proverbial heat and dust of a dangerous land where the lesser breeds were wilfully hell-bent on obstructing the progress of the Empire, and good natives were the ones who showed a doglike devotion to the white man. Churchill's oratory referred to a patch of pink on the map belonging to His Majesty the King Emperor. And then there was the procession of visitors from Katherine Mayo to Beverly Nichols who between teatime and cocktails pronounced their own weighty little verdicts on India. The vocabulary of colonial discourse was stocked with heavy, rock-solid phrases such as 'the subject races' and words like 'heathen', which assumed a perfectly natural division of the world into rulers and ruled, and took for granted the power relationships of the time, of class, of colour and of race. Our interpreters actually spoke and wrote these words and phrases in all earnestness. The British Foreign Office drafted documents and conducted policy in this officialese. Colonial literature and cinema grew out of them, portraying a Never Never Land of horrid Eastern villainy and handsome Western virtue. In the film called *Gunga Din,* Douglas Fairbanks Jr and Cary Grant battled heroically with a band of Indian thugs led by a wicked old thug made up to resemble Mahatma Gandhi. And Indian news reached the outside world suitably selected and doctored by the government. Mass upsurges became 'unrest', and could take second place to important items such as the fact that the maharaja of Mysore had shot a 900lb tiger. The interpreters added their own hardy building blocks to this edifice of imperial language. Immortal among these are Kipling's description of the lesser breeds as 'half devil and half child' and Churchill's divinely ordained 'mission of Christendom' and 'the mission of the English-speaking peoples'.

The mythology of the Empire created by this language dies hard, which may explain the long-lasting Raj nostalgia, whereas nobody has given a second thought to the Dutch or Portuguese empires which had no comparable supporting mystique, and remained brisk, businesslike affairs of conquest and profit. They had nothing resembling Land of Hope and Glory, that emotive combination of hymn and battle cry, glorifying conquest and sanctifying occupation with God's blessing. Imperial language regarded Christianity and Christian scripture as its indispensable ally, God had a starring role in the whole enterprise, and it was Christian soldiers who marched to extend the frontiers of the Empire. Thus we were reduced by this language to figments of the Anglo-Saxon imagination. Even a child felt harrowed and puzzled by it, up against a mythical orient created by the writers, historians and other upholders of the Raj. Which was real, I kept asking myself, me or they, for it was clear that we both could not be.

It is the triumph of any mystique that it looks as if it partakes of eternity, that it is as undeniable and elemental as a fact of nature – whether it is the feminine mystique or empire – when of course it is nothing of the kind, and only needs a different arrangement of words on a page to start undoing it, along with all the images and stereotypes it invented. And the British Empire began to be undone as words began to be differently arranged on a page, taking us out of the stranglehold of the imperial point of view. After Independence, the intermediary was eliminated, and Churchill's 'mission of the English-speaking peoples' became the radically different mission of people of all climes and colours who had made English their own. And Europe has now recognized this development, and rewarded it with last year's Nobel Prize for Literature, and with the Peace Prize, to representatives of people colonized and dispossessed by the white man. It is a long way from Kipling to Derek Walcott and Rigoberta Menchu, and one might say the wheel has come full circle, but has it? How much difference can prizes make to the great structures of power that still control us? Or the kind of people we have become as the result of a particular past? There *is* a postmodern East, but some of its best and worst features mirror the postmodern West.

Let's take the East–West encounter, as this collision of cultures, this seizure of land and resources, establishment of hegemony and deprival of dignity is called. It is still a fact of our life, our politics, our character, our literature, as anything that happens to one continues to be. We are indelibly shaped by it. We are still maimed and scarred by it, aroused to anger, admiration or imitation by it. It remains an ineradicable experience, and our most recent frame of reference: The complexity of this (or probably any) encounter lies in the fact that it was not all of a piece. The responses to it were many and various. Some gave their lives to the struggle for freedom from British rule; others supported and served the Raj and reaped the knighthoods and rewards of its loyal servants; for the majority it may well have been one more experience of new masters, this time under a more crushing burden of exploitation. And it was not all of a piece even for an individual. Love and hate, opposition and friendship, rejection and adoption could all engage the same human heart. The British added one more complex layer to Indian identity and we are still sorting out the fallout of this last top layer.

But who really are 'we'? At one end of the spectrum is a majority who still cannot write, and have yet to write their experience. So present writing may well be an elite rehearsal for the more representative performance yet to come once *these* Indians – which means *most* Indians – can express themselves directly. Their expression will be less allied to Western taste, patronage and publication, and it may reveal an identity very different from the one we fancy ourselves as having today. Over four decades of universal suffrage have made this grass-roots identity very decisive and tumultuous in the political process, but it still has to surface in literature. At the other end of the spectrum are the very rich, who for all practical purposes have seceded from India, even if they remain in India as Indian nationals. As far as their goals, their interests, and even their material arrangements are concerned, they have pulled out and have much less to do with India than with their counterparts in the West. And the implications of the social and economic fragmentation this has brought about are as devastating in their impact on the country as of those who want India's boundaries redrawn. India's two economies, the vulgar ostentation and growing consumerism on the one hand and a continuing and even growing impoverishment on the other, are a sign of the complete separation between the rich and the poor. It used to be said the poor had no nation. They have been, and still are, lured or dragged across continents to provide labour. Now it is the rich who have no nation and no loyalty, except to money.

Between these two extremes lies an India where the very meaning of 'India' is now the cause of slaughter and debate, and where the assertion of identity is taking the form of demands for greater autonomy, or outright secession from the Union, some fuelled by Muslim or Sikh religious fundamentalism, while Hindu fundamentalism wants to preserve unity by bottling and pickling India in an exclusive Hindu mould and clamping it into a fixed unchanging identity. To start conceiving India as the cultural monopoly of Hindus, with every other culture on Indian soil seen as an imposter and outsider, would not only be a radical departure from the cardinal principles that went into the making of modern India, but a misrepresentation of Indian history and an abuse of cultural memory. It would result in a shrunken, artificial self-image made up of selected racial memories. It would deal a death blow to my own cherished sense of Indianness, whose very essence is its ethnic and religious diversity and its cultural plurality. But this is the kind of death blow many like myself are now facing in India, with mystical dreams and blood urges dictating what nationality should mean.

It I may give a personal illustration, I cannot help being acutely aware of the danger of this lethal combination of nationalism and religion, for it has blown two members of my own family to shreds, leaving almost nothing of their mortal remains to cremate at their state funerals.

Then there are the writers, those who explain us to ourselves and to the world. Many of those who write in English live and write in the West. They are not affected by the raw winds assailing India or – which is more crucial – by the texture of daily life. They are not encumbered by the nitty-gritty of carving out a continuity from difficult, sometimes unpredictable, circumstances, with gaining an inch of breathing space at a time in the ongoing process of building a nation that has only in recent times become a nation.

They live in circumstances so materially and psychologically removed from those of their countrymen on the subcontinent as to give them almost nothing in common – least of all an identity – connected with hailing from the same piece of territory on a map. They are reacting to the pressures and concerns of an environment that is not Indian, and are fashioning identities born of choice, not of history.

And then, who we are is further complicated by the fact that the West is still The World, and we are more shadow than substance in conditions where the West dominates industry and capital, technology, finance, information and trade; where no sovereign authority is allowed to interfere with the laws or the lawlessness of the market; and with the collapse of the Soviet Union there is now no countervailing ideology in politics or economics to act as a brake on it. It used to be the Empire that told us who we were. Now it is this new empire, of managers of the global economy, who warn us we will have no existence unless we toe the line, while the marketers of images tell us we have no identity but the one they choose to impose on us. At another level, literature, like everything else in this postmodern age, toes the line too when the deconstructionists tell us the same thing, that interpretation is the experience, that every written word and sentence has to be decoded, and has no existence unless it is decoded. And perhaps this would distort us less if all decoding did not proceed from European insights, European cultural traditions and European approaches to rationality and logic.

Few things have been more destabilizing for millions of people across the globe and for their concept of identity than this imperialism in a new garb. It axes the roots, and cuts off the blood supply, of ancient systems of thought, of the oldest values known to mankind – of community, sharing and concern for the weak and vulnerable. It rides roughshod over a view of life older then the hills whose health and harmony depended on taking the whole universe outside oneself into consideration.

These are cultural values that were first threatened during the era of colonial domination, when they began to be challenged through processes of development and modernization which, in effect, meant westernization. 'Do like we do,' the West declares, 'and you'll be rich like us.' So *Rich Like Us* was the title I gave to a novel of mine in which a fizzy drink called Happyrola allies itself with local corruption and a dynastic dictatorship to launch India into modern times. The West's is still the dominant and domineering culture. The world is still seen through its cultural lenses, analysed through its modes of thought and prescribed the remedies Europe thinks best. Imposing the Western agenda has often meant psychological disorientation, physical dislocation and political tumult as systems alien to the West struggle to provide goods they cannot possibly provide, for people who cannot afford to buy them and would not know how to use them. The result has been enrichment at one end and abysmal poverty at the other. An all-powerful market that allows nothing to stand in the way of its access to commodities that will maintain the lifestyle of the world's most privileged people has thought nothing of going to total war for the purpose, as it did in the Gulf most recently. Its capture of forests and minerals and other natural resources has forced people to migrate to already overburdened cities because their resources and all their familiar comforting patterns of life are wrenched away. Their notions of identity are thrown into a flat spin, and this has made them recruits for whatever illusory identities are on offer. And the fact that this kind of volcanic upheaval is on must make all talk of identity in a lecture hall, or discussion about it at literary conferences, as far removed from what is actually happening as Marie Antoinette's hairstyle from the business end of a guillotine. But that kind of yawning chasm is frequently present in situations where the book, the text, the theory, take precedence over life and humanity, and when high priests act as intermediaries between man and his salvation, especially when the high priests are grafting their own somewhat blinkered vision on it.

It could be this ruthless encroaching tide of alien values that helps tip cultures backwards into the cauldron of fundamentalism, in order to resist it, and save themselves from being bulldozed in a direction they don't want to go. When they think about the centuries of Christian power and the disasters that Christianity, as interpreted by the West, have visited on mankind, from crusades and genocides to the millions of corpses piled up in two major and countless minor wars, they may not think it a very good idea to make themselves in the Western image, apart from their objections to what the West regards as worthwhile personal goals. This veritable onslaught of a Western lifestyle may be helping to breed a nostalgia for a past that may well be mythical, but is no less powerful on that account. It may be helping to drive societies back to a way of life, good or bad, but rooted in their own history; or goading groups within societies to aggrandize religion, or to seek refuge in smaller sub-national identities – all of which may be remedies much worse than the disease they are fleeing from, but do look like havens in a storm. Ironically enough, the multiculturist policy in Britain, which seeks in good faith to understand and accommodate other cultures, sometimes ends up supporting the obscurantist elements of those cultures, and encourages pockets of medievalism whose spokesmen and defenders are men, leaving women to start their struggles for freedom from scratch and not allowing them to routinely benefit from the liberal social environment they are living in. In this respect, the multiculturist policy resembles our imperial interpreters who used to promote the archaic, the quaint and the exotic as the genuine article and true representative of a culture, when true tradition is not static, but something we make and unmake by our sweat and toil as we go along.

I confess I am ill-equipped by background and temperament to appreciate the world of modern-day no-holds-barred capitalism assisted by rapidly changing technology, having been brought up to the view that a politics or an economics, a private or a public life, motivated solely by self-interest and self-satisfaction was one that could only degenerate into greed, grab and lunacy. I grew up, of course, in rare times, as any atmosphere created by the striving for freedom always is. I realize that ordinary life does not often breed or sustain such an atmosphere. My own novels are about how the idealism of an emergent nation has withered and rotted in corruption and decay. But I am tainted by those rarefied times and cannot shed them any more than I can my skin, and so I hobble about some areas of the postmodern world, this world they tell me is the real world, which somehow looks strangely unreal to me. Oh, I can see it is there. What I want to know is, is it true? I have to keep asking myself as I did in childhood of the solid, undeniable empire that surrounded, pervaded and ruled us, is it real, or am I, because we both cannot be. So when they tell me what I see around me is the new reality we must accept and pay homage to, I've heard that story before. Believe it, they say, the old ideas have been overthrown, there is no scheme of things but this. Fit into it or die. But for me it is the old tricky question of illusion and reality once again. Seeing is not always believing, and very far from accepting. I know the landscape flashing past is really standing still, and that my own reckoning has to be with its eternities, and not with the brute, literal fact that I am being propelled past it, rushed in a direction I don't want to travel.

Anyway, I ask myself, how is this direction they want to rush me in any different from all the rampaging fundamentalisms that are tearing sanity to bits? Isn't this inflexible, intractable Western grip on the world with its well-intentioned diktat: Be reasonable, do it my way; or: Do like we do and you'll be rich like us; isn't this a form of fundamentalism that non-westerners have been facing since Christopher Columbus, when life on the planet began to be savagely, or benevolently, but in any case methodically, refashioned in the Western image? Haven't we lived in the fundamentalist climate of the West's own non-negotiable revelations of the truth?

One of these, communism, they say for some reason is now 'over'. The other, which they call economic know-how and the supremacy of the market, is now supposed to be the road to salvation. Yet it hasn't even the grace of the old imperialism, for the old imperialist was on the spot. He had responsibilities to fulfil, he was accountable to his Parliament. He was a human being whose face we saw and whom we dealt with at a hundred human levels, with all the give and take that involved, albeit as unequals. The new imperialism is an absentee push-button affair and involves no human process at all, only profits.

Of course I'm slow to understand the advantages of this New Age, from its political and economic priorities to the marvels of its technology. In an age of expertise I'm not an expert on anything and I know nothing about the formulae that make the world go round. I've opted out of the latest model, whatever it might be. I try never to be in fashion. I'm so untrendy I even live in India, instead of somewhere more congenial where things work and creature comforts are not in short supply. I don't write about caste, joint family or picturesque ethnicity. I'm more interested in trying to trace in human terms the implications of what happens to us politically, the ideas and behaviour that religion breeds in us, and my ongoing character has been India. I've never used an electric typewriter, because where I live, electricity is apt to be cut off in the middle of a sentence for a couple of hours. Nor do I use a word processor. I've always believed words were processed in a cavern in one's brain, and flowed on to paper straight from there. My town hasn't caught up with the communications revolution and my telephone does me a favour when it works, so it was quite a feat serving on the jury of the Commonwealth Writers' Prize for two years, and keeping in close touch with the judging centres at Sydney and Toronto. So I'm the last person who should be talking to you about the times we live in. A couple of years ago at a literary conference in Hongkong where writers talked about their methods of composing, a young Welsh poet said that word processors were such a remarkable invention that he even found his style changing when he started to use one. But as I plan to stick to my style, this decided me finally against ever using one. And as to methods of composing, I doubt I'll ever find one as good as staring out of the window. I'm backward in other ways too. I feel dreadfully out of step with the times when I come across thousand-page novels or somebody's life in six volumes. I don't buy them because I can't stagger home with them, or relax in bed with them, but also because floods of words, like affluence beyond a point, or speed beyond a point, leave me stunned and stupid. It may also be that I have a natural bent for brevity and for leaving *out* as much as I can. It may be my way of countering the explosion of verbiage that has hit us, and the fact that pause, silence and emptiness are so little valued for the power they possess. The best thing about a novel used to be that no one had to read it. It might be something one discovered on a bookshelf all by oneself, a treasure awaiting discovery, perhaps long after it was written. But now, the publicity, the hype, the commerce surrounding it are so relentless, that this most magical way of passing one's time has been relegated like all else – like music, art and sport – to merchandise, and ourselves to one more form of bombardment.

I'm also bewildered by all the intimidating theories about writing. I can see the point of analysing the physical world. Put a cross section of a leaf or a frog under a microscope and you've found out something about it that will hold good six months hence. But that's because they're dead. The writer who is cross-sectioned and analysed is not only still around, she's also changing. And writing is in part a mysterious process that must needs remain mysterious. In any event it's a risky business, and a thankless job, being an intermediary, as I'm sure the Pope must have discovered when the Reformation began. And I've wondered if this extent of dissection of texts doesn't make writers, readers and reviewers self-conscious? Just as the Welsh poet's computer was spawning a new style, are the critics and analysts spawning style? Do readers crouch in wait for hidden meanings, and writers labour to supply ever more 'special effects'? The truth may be far more simple, far less contorted and acrobatic. Yet the whole business of making sense of anything seems to have passed into a maze from which it will never emerge. Instead of saying: Row, row, row your boat gently down the stream, we seem to be saying: Propel, propel, propel your craft languidly down the liquid solution. And at the end of all these contortions the experts seem to have come up with the melancholy conclusion that we are spinning without a centre, that in this postmodern era there is no fixed meaning to anything since everything, including identity, keeps changing, and every shift is subject to many interpretations.

Another thing I can't seem to catch up with is the vogue for telling it all. We are repeatedly reminded – in case we may have forgotten – of the behaviour of bodies in bed. Now I think what is being celebrated by all this compulsive repetition and description, in books and cinema, is possibly the rediscovery by Christians that there's no such thing as original sin. And of course that's great news. But the Renaissance celebrated it so much more interestingly. It produced not only a wealth of magnificent nudes, but a wealth of investigation into scientific and natural phenomena, in short an expansion of knowledge and the whole human consciousness, which resulted in a new way of looking at life. This time round the celebration seems to be stuck with coitus and climax. But maybe this has something to do with the word processor.

To go on with my misfit condition, I have trouble convincing myself that the all-powerful market will bring us to the promised land of prosperity, since even in Toronto a year ago – which is one of the world's wealthiest cities – I had only to walk out of the plush hotel I was put up in to see a line of beggars in rags holding out their hats for coins. Yet it seems to me as foolish to say that capitalism has failed because I saw beggars in Toronto, and see them here in Britain, as that communism has failed. No system that succeeded in educating millions, compressing centuries of growth into a quarter-century, and fiercely defending its soil in a world war as communism did, can be said to have failed. What has failed is the capacity of these two Western gospels to understand and make room for each other, and profit by an intelligent combination of the two. Why should it be impossible for people to take the best of all human experience – this common human ancestor – into their blueprints for the future?

When I hear that communism is 'over', as many say that religion is 'over', I wonder if anything can be over that has once happened to us, and has jerked or stretched our awareness to the smallest degree? I am not a communist or any other -ist, but I do know what it did for a society like India – and probably for the world – was serve as a conscience-awakener. If communism triumphed at all, it is because it would have taken another hundred years for any other idea to break through the bastions of caste, class and privilege. Here's what the words 'You have nothing to lose but your chains' did for a character named Sonali in my novel *Rich Like Us.* And I quote:

> I wrote that sentence in large capitals in one of my notebooks to keep its lilting promise before me. Why had nobody, nobody at all, put those words together in exactly this eight-word formation before? . . . It unlocked a small high window in my mind, an unused attic window, and air rushed in to swirl old scraps and particles around in a blizzard of dust, settling them after the storm in strange new configurations . . . . A sightless beggar reflected in the glass show window of a shop displaying highheeled snakeskin shoes. Baby brides taking their dolls with them to their husbands' homes. My attic window gave me an anguished awareness I would never have had, though all that I became aware of at one stroke had been as if forever present in my consciousness.

What more is there to say except that it is through this deepening, expanding, metamorphosing consciousness that identity takes a beating, or blossoms, and is perpetually renewed and reshaped. Through this open awareness historians reinterpret history and people everywhere continually reinvent themselves. We are not what we were yesterday, or what we will be tomorrow. But our intelligent recycling of whatever happens to us, the human race – either individually or collectively – can help us transcend even the most brutal and agonizing of these experiences, and transform them into patterns ever more human and humane. As I wrote this, a literary example came to mind: Ishiguro's novel *The End of the Day.* When I read this I thought how seamless an example of interwoven identities it was; how identity in this case had resolved itself flawlessly through art; how British, and yet how exquisitely noiseless and Japanese a novel it was; and with so perfect an end product, how utterly irrelevant was the question of Ishiguro's identity.

As an Indian I am a mix of cultures and influences, of Hinduism, Islam and Christianity, of East and West. The interplay of a variety of historical and educational factors in my upbringing should perhaps have torn me apart, made me unsure of my identity and driven me to seek some simple answer to the question: who am I? Curiously enough, it has had the opposite effect. I have learned to make the most of my cultural confusion and to regard it as a blessing, not a curse. The act of writing has given me, besides, the opportunity to look critically at some of the formidable bastions of identity we base our lives on – nation, class, family. I have had occasion to publicly oppose the dynastic ambition of my family, and the brief dictatorship over which it presided, and to discover that the labels others know us by are not what we are. I've come to understand that what I am instead, is a writer. Any narrower identity separate from writing gradually disappears into the words one puts on a page, until eventually 'writer' is the only name tag that fits. A woman, an Indian, a citizen of the world – in the course of a lifetime one is many things – but not until I had shaken off the labels others had given me, become a cheerful traitor to my origins, unlearned much I had been taught, and put experience together quite differently in words on a page, did I know who I was.

To get back to the meditation technique I began with, one is born, according to the Hindus, in order to realize oneself. The sages did not mean the writing process, but perhaps there's no better way to make a start.

I don't know about you, but I'm not spinning without a centre. Nor do I feel there is no sense to be made of anything because the centre does not hold. Mine holds, maybe because I am not in the state of advanced modernity categorized as postmodern. I'm not European, and so I don't have to go by Europe's categories, or squash myself into Europe's conceptual and cultural scheme of things, its bare minimum field of facts and data accessible to scientific research, its dependence on the material for explanations, its gung-ho physical emphasis. There are other ideas and approaches that merit study in their own right. There is a whole other universe of value waiting to come to light which does not lend itself to definition in European terms, or *on* European terms. And it will, the day the white man lays down his burden and holds out his hand in equal partnership. For it is too diverse a world for one angle of vision to explain it, and one set of conclusions to decide how it should be run. There must be creative compromises possible between here and now and the hereafter. It may be time for the *West* to strike it rich by acknowledging other angles of vision, and by using other keys to open up its own culture to new definition. Quite a lot – including its own construct of postmodern identity – that reduced and undernourished consciousness which plays second fiddle to technology, biology, chemistry, commerce and manufacture – may begin to be sorted out in the process. Only in the give and take of a more egalitarian climate can we begin gratefully to recognize what we owe each other, and only then can we justly celebrate our combined, stupendous human heritage, and partake of a truly common identity.

The Schizophrenic Imagination*

I am a little dazzled, and more than a little intimidated, by all the scholarship I have heard propounded in the last few days. I have also wondered when 'post-colonial' is supposed to end. First we were colonials, and now we seem to be post-colonials. So is 'colonial' the new Anno Domini from which events are to be everlastingly measured? My own awareness as a writer reaches back to x-thousand BC, at the very end of which measureless, timeless time the British came and stayed and left. And now they're gone and their residue is simply one more layer added to the layer upon layer of Indian consciousness. Just one more.

The title of my talk may be misleading in terms of studies made about the subject – ofwhich I know nothing. So let me begin by explaining that I am thinking of schizophrenia as a state of mind and feeling that is firmly rooted in a particular subsoil, but above ground has a more fluid identity that doesn't fit comfortably into any single mould. A schizophrenic of this description is a migrant who may never have left his people or his soil. We are all somewhat divided selves, but I'm referring to the divisions that history and circumstance impose on the complex creatures we already are. Let me take the example of Jawaharlal Nehru, a product of colonial

* Plenary Address at ACLALS Conference, University of Kent, Canterbury, 30 August 1989. Published in *Wasafiri*, No. 11, Spring 1990 and in *Unbecoming Daughter of the Empire*, Dangaroo Press, 1993.

times who called himself a man of two worlds, but unlike the quotation describing one of these as dead, the other powerless to be born, both his worlds were alive and vigorous. He was not in any limbo. That was the trouble. His was a life lived in two-plus-one cultures, in many ways a story of assimilation, yet the times he lived in and the role he played in them placed his cultures in conflict and confrontation. The struggle for independence gave the conflict a historic setting, and his life and personality a very different direction from the one it would otherwise have taken.

Educated Indians had, of course, been in contact with Western civilization since the British occupation, though most Indians, who lived by the sun, the rain and the seasons were not touched by it. But many of the educated too were affected only in their outer lives. It had not become second nature except for those few whose class and opportunities made this possible. Of these, some related to the East–West encounter by discarding their Indianness to become brown carriers of the white culture they admired and adopted. But nationalism produced another breed of westernized Indian for whom his plural culture meant a bewildering reckoning with himself, a balancing act, where the priorities were never in doubt, but where 'Who am I?' remained an ongoing search and question. Nehru was one such Indian, and it may be that many of his countrymen and women are still sorting out the meaning of this particular historical experience.

In contrast, Nirad Chaudhuri, a man of the same generation as Nehru, born when the words empire and colonial still had benign associations, seems not only an unanguished product of the same period, but one who became a philosophical observer and erudite chronicler of the colonial framework he was born and bred in. After Independence, at an advanced age, when few people emigrate of choice to set up house and put down roots somewhere else, he could leave India never to return, and could flourish heart-whole in what perhaps was, and is, the real country of his imagination, teaching the English how to stay English. For those who did not cross swords with the imperial order, it was simply the order of the day. For many it had a mystique, the elemental rightness, and right to be there, of a natural phenomenon.

A strong element of mystique attached to Nehru's outlook too, but it was the mystique of the fight for freedom, though that is not all it was. It was also traceable to his peculiar involvement with India, as fact, as dream, and as possibility. He wrote in *Discovery of India:* 'For we are very old, and trackless centuries whisper in our ears.' He was aware of that whisper. One incident towards the end of his life sums up the quality of his involvement. The family was at the breakfast table. A nephew said the country was in a mess, its problems would never be solved, and he, for one, was getting out to settle abroad. Nehru's daughter was listening sympathetically. Suddenly Nehru who had remained silent, spoke in a rage, 'Go where you like, but if I am born a thousand times, a thousand times I will be born an Indian.' It was a statement of almost mystical emotion and power. It had an echo of the cult of the motherland, for in the early years of this century these had been the last words of more than one Indian martyr after he mounted the gallows for his execution. This was Nehru's subsoil speaking though he was a man deeply identified with other nationalisms, as also with the science, learning and pleasures of the West, and was better known as an internationalist than perhaps any other figure of his time. He was also saying that to transform your society, you have to be in it. The ultimate battles, whether for freedom or after it, are fought on your own soil. He was implying 'My life is my message,' as opposed to 'My text is my message.' But the impassioned ingredient in his make-up is common to those everywhere – from rebels against empire to iconoclasts in art and literature – who see that there are facts which must be denied, and that there is more than one way of looking at the world.

There is a story from the imperial era about an Englishman whose posting in the Sudan was over. He was to leave with his family for England and he was pleased when his little son begged to be taken to say goodbye to the statue of Gordon. The father was proud that his child remembered all he had been taught about General Gordon's magnificent defence of Khartoum, a heroic event in the annals of Empire, and was deeply moved when tears ran down the child's face as they stood at the famous equestrian statue, until the boy asked, 'Daddy, who's that man sitting on Gordon?' It is those who in all honesty and earnestness are looking at the horse and not the rider, who can fit neatly into no tradition except one that is in the making. If anyone wants to fit me into a tradition, it is this tradition-in-the-making they will have to settle for.

My own divided experience starts with belonging to north India, a region that has been spared no convulsion or folk experience, from epic marvels and a matchless metaphysics to repeated invasion and slaughter. My part of the Ganga plain is the cradle of Hinduism but it is home to Islam as well, and Indo-English by virtue of the continuing impact and fallout of British rule. All three influences meet in the city of my birth whose original name, Prayag, figures in the Ramayana, while its present name, Allahabad, testifies to Muslim conquest and rule, and where every road in my childhood was named after an Englishman, the public park had a statue of stout old Queen Victoria, and down the road from our house two nights a week came dance music from a club that did not admit Indians.

Going to school was like arriving at the club that didn't admit Indians. My school admitted Indians but ignored India. As I was quite sure that India existed, I didn't place much faith in school. At home I was nourished on revolt. My elders were committed to rooting out foreign rule and had made a personal beginning by giving up their scholarship and their careers at the Bar to devote their lives and all their resources to the struggle for freedom. They were so enthralled with organizing for it, and being imprisoned for it, that I thought going to jail was a career. They had no regular incomes because they had given up their means of livelihood, but they found it so exhilarating doing without the comforts, amenities and certainties other people took for granted, that when I was introduced to what is known as normal life after Independence, it gave me quite a shock with its very different priorities. I had never before met people who earned a living, took holidays, joined clubs, went shopping and knew what tomorrow would bring, and they struck me as a quaint and exotic species. Above all, the whole business of entertaining, of serving elaborate meals to other well-fed people, and then going to *their* houses to be fed elaborate meals by *them*, seemed to me an extremely curious way of spending time. There are several aspects of normal life I still haven't got used to. I think I started to write books as a retreat from it. I know I am ill-equipped to be part of normal life. I will forever be an outsider looking in through its windows, marvelling at the sequences and continuities of normal life. When I try to read them, they look like hieroglyphics, a fascinating language for which I lack the code.

In a childhood filled with the sights, sounds and folklore, and sometimes the furor, of the national movement, nothing estranged me from school more than the way history was taught. Its content and perspective were so different from what I learned at home that I soon put school history in the same category as Kipling's *Gunga Din* – a rousing, rollicking white man's fable that had everything to do with the conqueror's image of the bullied, beaten Indian, loyal to his last gasp, and nothing to do with India. In short I didn't believe a word of it. I was also surprised to learn that ancient times began with Greece, that the world had been created in six days, and that all of religion was down in one little book. Though the nuns did their best with me, privately I suspected that God Almighty was my grandfather, and Jesus Christ must be my uncle, since he carried other people's sorrows on his back; that they, together with my father and mother, were special shining beings, and that the fight for freedom was the path to the Holy Grail. I knew I inhabited a huger, older universe of which school taught me only a meagre slice, yet paradoxically this little scrap filled the textbooks and ruled the world.

Home had its paradoxes too, but they fell into place as part of a larger purpose. I can see my frail, spectacled, widowed grandmother sitting cross-legged on her bedroom floor reading in a low mutter from her enormous large-print Ramayana, and shrieking for a servant when a mouse darts across the floor, but she's the same woman who picketed foreign cloth shops not long before, and who once stayed firmly put at the head of a procession halted by the police. Let me quote what happened next from a written account. She was 'knocked down … and hit repeatedly on the head with canes. Blood came out of an open wound in her head; she fainted and lay on the roadside.' Within these outer tensions there were inner tensions, for non-violence does not come naturally to the human race, and my father once got solitary confinement for knocking down a jail guard who insulted my grandmother when she visited him in jail. I used to wish the time would come when my parents would stay home like other parents. For one of them the time never came, for my father died of his last imprisonment. I'm not sure whether a childhood lived in this heightened state of national and world awareness was euphoric or wretched. It is probably best described by Pushkin's reaction when he read Gogol's *Dead Souls.* After laughing uproariously all the way through it, he exclaimed, 'Oh God, how sad our Russia is!' It has been said that a person who survives her childhood has enough information to last her for the rest of her days, and it must be true, or my novels would not have reflected the political idealism of an emergent nation, and its progressive destruction and decay. There is always an obstinate idealist hanging around in my fiction, usually with as much chance of success or survival as a snowball in Hades.

I did not set out to write 'political fiction'. I have no ideology except a vague sort that feels uncomfortable with title and privilege, with kings, queens and political dynasties. I have no message either, unless it is the non-message that Europe is not the centre of the world. Politics for me was an environment in which every issue was a political issue, and personal and political fates were inextricably bound. If it has remained a continuing awareness, it is because I live in an unsettled order, one I am trying to change, one where I am witness to the public and domestic misuses of power. And politics was for so long dictated by other people's view of us, that I have found it satisfying to give it Indian expression and interpretation. Yet, though I use a political backdrop or events – since these happen to be the outer focal points that trigger my imagination, and also because I think we gain or lose significance in our relationship to events – I prefer to think of my fiction as having a sense of history, in a country where race, religion or caste can decide the course of a love affair, where it can take as much raw courage to choose a husband, or leave him, as to face a firing squad. The nuclear family with its attendant traumas is not for us. Our traumas like our families are built on a grander scale. From where I stand, looking at the horse and not the rider, it doesn't seem to me there *is* such a thing as a purely individual predicament. Too many other factors blur and burden it, including the weather. Fornication and adultery go on in India as anywhere else, but I'm not sure they can be given such free rein as in Western fiction without becoming unrelated to a social condition where the individual is tied hand and foot, and often back-breakingly, to wider responsibility. For one thing he hasn't got the time. And she has even less. But as we approach Western living conditions – as in my novel after next – there will be more time for adultery.

Then, societies that have lived long under foreign domination bring their own behaviour characteristics into play. Passivity can become an active choice, a strength, among people where invasion and reconquest have been the pattern, because it is one's best chance of remaining whole. Sycophancy too is the hallmark of the survivor and all cultures have sycophants. But when I wonder why *we* produce them in such abundance – and this struck me strongly during the 1975-77 dictatorship known as the Emergency – then I have to ask, as I did in my novel *Rich Like Us*, whether Hinduism inclines a whole society to the status quo. Does it put out the fires of rebellion? Does it incline women to victimization, to individual and mass acts of horrifying self-sacrifice? Has the cult of virtue (female) and honour (male) been so ferocious and merciless in any other society that prides itself on its humane values? How do we explain this aspect of ourselves? I have been much preoccupied with the effects of Hinduism on character in my novels.

All Indians are not Hindus but all Indians must reckon with Hinduism since it is the dominant setting, the social and psychological atmosphere. Yet what it is we are reckoning with is hard to say when Hinduism has no beginning, no founder, no church, no commandments, no single Bible, no single prophet or messiah. There can never be a law of blasphemy against Hinduism, or any other concrete religious measure to bring all Hindus into line. But memory and imagination are much the most powerful of human possessions, and give us almost unlimited scope for both enlightenment and bigotry. This, then, is the sky my characters and I live under, and in one sense I am nothing if I am not a Hindu. On the Indian subcontinent there is no escape from the aspect of cultural behaviour we call religious.

Some Hindus solve their problem of how to come to terms with Hinduism by dumping it and calling themselves atheists, agnostics or secular. But this is no solution for a writer. If I change my name today to Henrietta von Blinkenstaff, whom am I trying to fool? Can I quick-change my bones, my myths or my grandparents? Can I forget that my great-grandmother became a sati? So I find it more useful to say, Believe it, you are a Hindu. Now figure out, if you can, what that means, and fiction is part of the process of figuring it out. Even if I were so inclined, it would be futile to wish away a force that has moulded hundreds of generations, that governs some countries, and is a governing force in others, and whose absolutism has crossed national frontiers to sentence a writer to death for blasphemy. There is no safe distance from such a force, any more than there is from modern weaponry. Literature can hardly ignore this unfinished question.

I used to try to integrate my overpowering heritage, feel relaxed and easy about it, but I've discovered I'm not supposed to feel integrated and relaxed. It is not only inevitable, it is also perfectly natural for the inheritor of one of the earth's oldest and most complex inheritances to feel fragmented. And I have learned to treat my own particular muddle as a priceless asset. It is for my third eye to reconcile these fragments through fiction, and through my sense of a plural self to produce a fiction other than that which a less ancient, more homogeneous, more settled society produces. Time itself – an important event of the novel – is not the same in the Indian, especially the Hindu, reckoning as in other societies, including other ancient societies that have suffered uprooting shocks and made clean breaks with the past. The city I grew up in had coexisting time zones. The past is so much with us, in the beliefs and routines people live by, in conversations whose allusions can go from legend to modern in minutes, that no time is ever entirely past. It is modern times that strain my own imagination, and I don't think anyone has succeeded in creating a modern Indian character, if by 'modern' we mean a basic alteration or transformation from what went before. I'm not sure such a creature exists, so real life cannot be much help in providing examples. Is 'modern' the frame of mind that descends from the European Enlightenment? Is it the position you occupy in the race for European technology? Is the contemporary Western world still The World, and all other peoples to be judged by its yardsticks of progress? I've made some play with the word 'modern' in my last novel *Mistaken Identity*.

One of the effects of coming to terms with my own dividedness has been to ignore chronology and to free myself from Indian locale and characters in my fiction. This has been liberating for me, and I expect it must be so for schizophrenic fiction in general. Not only is it time for interpretation to flow many ways instead of only West to East, but the question of direction is itself no longer relevant when the migration of cultures is leaving cultures open-ended, and when migration can take place without ever leaving one's soil. Where does one culture begin and another end when they are housed in the same person? There are powerful winds blowing through English literature. English is being assaulted by cross-currents of racial experience, by a vast expansion of its frame of reference, by new uses of imagination and language. The day of pure literatures, like pure or ruling races, is over, and English, at least, is in a new flowering – one that expresses a vision, a vitality, an expansionism that Sir Francis Drake and other English gentlemen never dreamed they would be unleashing when they set sail on their swashbuckling adventures.

To end with let me give you an example of the schizophrenia I am talking about. My father, a Sanskrit scholar, a fairly arrogant Indian, and a dedicated freedom fighter who was to die of British imprisonment a few years later, wept when London was bombed in the blitz, and when Paris fell to Hitler's armies. His answer to the question 'Who am I?' would have been, 'I am a member of the human race – and all the rest is rhetoric.'

The Virtuous Woman*

My great-grandmother became a sati. Somewhere in Bambuli village on the coast of Ratnagiri there may still be a shrine to her. I remember being told this when I was a child and it made the kind of impression on me that reading about jauhar in Rajput annals had done, when queens and their retinues of hundreds had died in flames. It was something distant, a terrifying, thrilling spectacle connected with 'virtue' (female) and 'honour' (male). It was a blend of history–culture–religion wrapped in the sanctified, impenetrable dust that shrouds an artificially preserved, rather than a living, heritage. It was romance. What I never could connect it with was reality, though real enough women had done these things.

I didn't hear, nor did I ask, why my great-grandmother had done this. And the event lay dormant in my consciousness for years until the 1970s brought the Emergency, which gave me an anguished awareness of the freedoms we had taken so much for granted and so suddenly lost. For not until I lost mine did I realize that most of my fellow citizens, especially women, had never been able to exercise theirs, or indeed known they had any to lose. The Emergency gave birth to a movement for civil liberties, and newspapers afterwards began to report their terrible abuses and violations in towns as well as rural areas. We read that in 1975, in Delhi alone, some

* *The Tribune*, 24 December 1988

three hundred women were burned alive by greedy in-laws. It was then that my burned Maharashtrian ancestress became a woman of flesh and blood and began to haunt me, and finally appeared in the next novel I wrote, *Rich Like Us.* She who belonged to one of the most independent traditions to which Indian women are heir, she who had never known purdah or the forms of serfdom the north imposes on its women, could she have gone to the pyre of her own free will? Was she drugged, dragged, forced? Did she really prefer death to life? And if so, is this the gruesome death anyone would choose when there are quicker ways of dying? But then, of course, sati is not only an awesome ending to a life. It is a human sacrifice, and sacrifice entails ceremonial, spectacle, witnesses. And if it is by free will, that will is the result of conditioning since the cradle, in a scenario where male 'honour' and female 'virtue' are a cult, ferocious in its connotations and merciless in its demands.

Staying alive as a widow constituted an offence against these, leaving home constituted another, even in circumstances where home means humiliation, persecution, injury and, ultimately, death, as with the three hundred burned brides in Delhi and countless unregistered cases. For though the sati revival has been alarming enough to attract stringent new legislation, the commandment never to leave home is still absolute. And staying put is the sati equivalent humbly accepted by women in the tragic belief that there is no other choice. Female conditioning says you may on no account leave, that you may be thrown out. Tough luck.

I began, through the writing process, to unlearn all I had been taught, including that overpowering mix called history–culture–religion, and to discover who I was through the words I put on a page. While I was struggling with problems of personal emancipation, my fictional Rashmi, in *This Time of Morning,* achieved hers, leaving a marriage that had become an emotional wasteland. I was still struggling when Saroj in *Storm in Chandigarh* left her jealous, unreasonable, unfaithful husband, though she had two children and was heavily pregnant with her third. Of course, she took them with her. And by the time I had become a walkout/thrown-out combine, Simrit in *The Day in Shadow* had become one too, only with a whole horde of children – a number I left unspecified as against my three – showing that even this could be done. Later, Devi in *A Situation in New Delhi* and Sonali in *Rich Like Us* chose to live their achieving lives, independent of men.

But the stereotype rules most women's lives. The TV serials *Ramayana* and *Mahabharata* have done nothing to dispel it, and a good deal to refurbish it. They have stimulated no debate about why Rama who threw out his beloved wife is the example of perfect manhood, or why Gandhari who was moronic enough to keep her eyes bandaged because her husband was blind, is considered an ideal woman. Yet in the West, each new production of Greek tragedy interprets it afresh, each new *Hamlet* represents a contemporary quandary, and recently Lear became a Japanese. Even Jesus Christ is for any artist to interpret as he pleases, and faith is not defiled, nor Christianity reviled, if he is pictured as a human being with human desires. Why must Hinduism be kept in cotton wool? A unique opportunity has been lost in not retelling our epics with lessons for our times. The same old dust envelops them, and a reindoctrinated public stays drugged and docile while monstrous new temples are built to celebrate new satis, and riots break out at the alleged birthplace of Rama.

It is clear the epics can only be re-examined when women take charge of their lives, when they dissect the stories of the female sacrificial examples they have been taught to worship, and ask: Could she have done this of her own free will? And if so, what manner of horrifying social pressures created such a will? Through the rewriting women do, new Sitas and Savitris will arise, stripped of false sanctity and crowned with the human virtue of courage. Then at last we will know why they did what they did, and how their lone, remote struggles can help our search for identity and emancipation.

My New Novel: *The Day in Shadow**

One of the things this book is about is divorce. Som's is a hard, competitive, violent world and he thrives on it, while Simrit has been brought up with a different kind of awareness about what the world should be. Awareness – if you take that to mean the sensing of possibilities and sensitivity to what lies beyond your immediate insistent environment – is a kind of disease that grows with age. It makes you thinner-skinned as you grow older. The horny outer layers of conventional reaction, of your own safe place in the world, keep falling off, exposing more and more of the nerve beneath – and you begin to feel every current in your environment more keenly. If the currents don't rhyme with your inner make-up the experience can become very painful. Even if you have been numb and content for years, enclosed in a comfortable formula of living, you eventually find out it won't do. Awareness breaks through – uninvited, relentless – and you have to look it in the face.

This is what happens to Simrit in *The Day in Shadow.* Her marriage to Som has worked quite well for years. It has all the hallmarks of success: mutual attraction, money, prospects, and a sexual relationship that flowers during her pregnancies. That is why she goes on having children. But there comes a time when all these ingredients of success become the instruments of her

**The Hindustan Times,* 18 December 1971

torture. What goes wrong? Another man in her life? A change in Som? Frighteningly enough, the growing realization that life is an intensely personal confrontation. The way you live has to agree with your mental make-up and your emotions, your liver and your glands, and even sex is finally tied up with all of these. Simrit discovers: 'Sex was no more just sex than food was just food .... Once the edge was off hunger a meal had to be more than food. And once past its immediacy, sex had its visions too – of tenderness, of humour, of more than a physical act.'

It would have been easier to explain Simrit's divorce in terms of another man. Only I am sure her kind of break was more paralysing because it could not be explained so simply. Besides, lots of marriages survive adultery. It is a tension between couples, a way of life on which two people cannot agree, that becomes difficult to cope with.

Why write a novel about a divorce? Because writing of any sort helps to put your own world in order, all the shapeless, bewildering fragments of it. It helps you to figure out what is happening in and around you. And in this book I tried to figure our something that had happened to me – the shattering experience of divorce. There are things that will never be understood until they are written, and sometimes not even then. But writing helps the process. So Simrit turned out to be somewhat like me, even to being a writer, and very stupid about practical matters.

But I wanted to do more in this novel than convey this emotional holocaust and how it affects a woman. I wanted to show how even in a free country like ours where women are equal citizens, a woman can be criminally exploited without its creating a ripple. Again I am not speaking of any obvious, recognizable form of exploitation against which most people will naturally raise a cry. If a man beats his wife, for instance, hardly anyone will condone the fact. But if at divorce he inflicts a financial settlement on her that enslaves her with taxes and makes it impossible for her to make a decent living, no one will take any notice because this is the kind of beating where the blood and bruises don't show. But in addition – and this is the crux of the matter – nobody bothers about it even when they do. Simrit in this story finds she has to serve as a tax convenience for her ex-husband all her life, and that tied up in this way, she will never be able to make an adequate living for herself. An extraordinary state of affairs, yet nobody thinks so, neither the lawyer who drafted the settlement, nor the court that approved it, nor even Simrit herself when she signed it, womanlike, without understanding what it was all about. The worst part of it is that Simrit, like most women, can be casually exploited because she is so eminently exploitable. She is a passive creature to whom things happen. She is not part of the creating, acting world. Even when the enormity of the settlement is explained to her she cannot bring herself to believe it, much less to fight it. Divorce for women is almost a sin, and in expiation of her share of the guilt she stays mute and acquiescent over the settlement, willing to accept it as part of her karma. Simrit is symbolic of the Hindu race.

The story takes place in Delhi and I can never think of Delhi without thinking of politics, Parliament, India. All these come into the book and form a big part of it. Everything around the writer is material for a novel, but few settings are as dramatic as Delhi today. I don't mean the present war situation but the general political atmosphere. I believe we move in a different medium today and that the Indian future is no longer geared, as it once was, to an Indian past. Raj, to whom Simrit turns for help, is a member of Parliament, a man who believes in life, not karma, and tries to persuade Simrit to do the same. He has a Herculean task because Simrit is not an individual – she is a culture, a tradition, a patient, enduring passivity. This is not Hinduism, but it is what Hinduism has come to represent.

And this is the theme underlying the novel, that Hinduism must change, revitalize itself if Hindus are to become an active, positive breed with something to give the world, and not be swept away by alien tides. It may not be fashionable to talk of religion or to be a believer, but I have never been in the least concerned about fashions or conformity. I am a believer in the greatest and most comprehensive metaphysics known to man – Hinduism – and in its powerful potential to provide men and women with a buoyant base for action. The question is – and no novel can answer it – will we discover it in time?

PART TWO

What Others Say

My Hero: Nayantara Sahgal by Hari Kunzru*

There are many ways of being a writer, but I have always had a special admiration for those who seem to embody their time and place in some profound way. Nayantara Sahgal was born in 1927, the niece of Jawaharlal Nehru, India's first prime minister. Her mother, Vijaya Lakshmi Pandit, was India's first ambassador to the UN. There are photos of her as a young girl standing beside Gandhi as he goes to give a speech. Looking at the photos illustrating her defence of her uncle's political legacy, *Jawaharlal Nehru: Civilizing a Savage World,* you have the impression of an almost Zelig-like quality. She was in the room as India was transformed from colony, to a non-aligned would-be socialist state, to today's world power.

One of Sahgal's many admirable qualities is that she has never been blinded by her privilege. When her cousin Indira Gandhi suspended India's Constitution in what became known as the Emergency, Sahgal was one of her fiercest critics, publishing a stream of journalism condemning her. Sahgal's scheduled appointment as ambassador to Italy was cancelled and she was threatened in a variety of ways. Her fiction is informed by her politics, particularly the tradition of non-violence. Many of her

* *The Guardian*, 21 July 2012

characters find themselves in situations where personal and political morality become intertwined. In *Mistaken Identity*, a colonial-era playboy is wrongly accused of being a subversive. In *Rich Like Us*, two women discover the corruption of their elite social milieu.

These days India has moved far away from Nehru's vision. His socialism is condemned for leading to the 'licence raj' of excessive bureaucracy and stagnation. The economic boom has given legitimacy to strains of nationalism. Sahgal has emerged as a fierce critic of the corruption that goes along with India's current get-rich-quick culture. In her eighties, she is still a working writer, and an important political voice.

Letter from Kaye Soki*

Dear Nayantara,

It has been a great privilege to get to know you through our mutual love and support of Woodstock School. You have been a profound influence on generations of idealistic young Indians as well as those who love India and the truths she has upheld by her enduring example. You and your family are of a piece with that heritage – and your mother's life story is a testimony to the spirit behind the heritage. I must also say that your book *Plans for Departure* and its theme of rational love – the possibility that lovers could also be comrades and intellectual equals – met the need of my heart at a difficult time in my own personal journey.

May God continue to bless you!
Kaye Soki

---

* Acting principal, Woodstock School, Mussoorie, till 15 June 2008

Letter from Indira Choudhury

4B Abhishek
15 Raja S.C. Mullick Road,
Calcutta 700086
24 May 1998

Dear Tara Masi,

I meant to write this earlier. I just wanted to thank you for your lovely letter. I was in Delhi for too short a period to visit Teen Murti or the Parliamentary Museum. I shall certainly follow this up next time. Thank you so much for taking an interest in my work.

I also wanted to thank you for publishing *Relationship* which I have just finished reading. For our generation I think it is a particularly significant book. We who were children during the 1960s hardly know enough about the political turmoils, the social scenario, and of the struggle of individuals to hold on to what they cherish and value. Your book tells me of all this and more, and as I read I could only admire the courage, the strength that you both express. For many of my generation who are (only now) confronting the many difficulties of relationships, your book will certainly be inspirational.

On a lighter note, a friend reading your Preface was amazed at the number of letters you'd written each other over such a short period – and then added that the figure would probably increase a hundred times if there was e-mail! I don't agree. I much prefer handwritten lyrical letters to 'computerized' romance! Thank you again for making a part of your private life public and sharing it with us.

I hope both of you are well. I have just written to Gita a fortnight ago.

With best wishes,
Indira
Indira Choudhury
English Department, Jadavpur University

Letter from Harold Pinter

221 - 0233

52 Campden Hill Square London W8 7JR

Jan. 27. 90

Dear Nayantara

Crazy about Mistaken Identity. I think it's absolutely brilliant. Many congratulations. We both read it on holiday in Mauritius & it gave us such joy.

When are you here?

Love

Harold

Letter from Antonia Fraser

FROM LADY ANTONIA FRASER ~~PINTER~~ Tel: 01-221-7678
52 Campden Hill Square London W8 7JR

27 January 1990

My dear Nayantara,

Mistaken Identity has leapt instantly into the category of 'One of my favourite Books'. I cannot remember when I was so moved, fascinated, enchanted, entertained and finally moved again.

Thank you so much for sending it to us.

With best wishes
yours
Antonia

P.S. And Raija, the free spirit, one of my favourite characters!

Letter from Naomi Lazard

Naomi Lazard
61 Pantigo Road
Easthampton, N.Y. 11937
U. S. A.

August 28, 1986

Nayantara Sahgal
c/o Norton Publishers
500 Fifth Ave.
New York, N.Y. 10036

Dear Nayantara Sahgal,

I have just had the exciting experience of reading your novel, Rich Like Us, and I want to tell you immediately how wonderful I think that novel is. I go through such parched patches trying to find books like this one, haunt the libraries, religiously search the reviews each Sunday of The New York Times, etc. But it only happens very occasionally that I find something like Rich Like Us.

Now I must find your other books. I will be thorough and if they are here I will find them.

In the last few years, since 1979 to be exact, when I started the project of translating the poetry of Faiz Ahmed Faiz into English, I have become an avid reader of literature from the sub-continent. Ofcourse, I read Passage to India long ago, but knowing Faiz and speaking with him about India my imagination was stirred and I actively look for books from that country (and from Pakistan). I was never able to read that quartet by Scott (The Raj Quartet) because I never could plow through the prose.

The True Subject, my translations from Faiz, will be published by Princeton University Press in 1987. If you are interested I'll see to it that you receive a copy. If there is anything I can send you before then please let me know. In the meantime many congratulations and my gratitude for Rich Like Us.

Faithfully yours,

Naomi Lazard

Naomi Lazard

Letter from Conrad Rooks*

conrad rooks
film maker

145 Golf Links, New Delhi 110003, India
Telephone 617255
Telex

Feb. 28th 1986

Dear Nayantara –

How very kind of you to reply quickly I am dreaming about the project. We must do a synopsis and rough draft screenplay before I leave for Paris. Either you should come and stay here with my wife and I or I come to you as we will need 7 days to do our work.

No one will listen to us unless we have something concrete to show, and a sensible budget will be

* Conrad Rooks was planning to make a film of my novel *Plans for Departure*. His ill health prevented this film from happening.

mpossiable without a script. I hope we can do it on 50 lac's "Ray" did his last film with Victor Banerjee for 40 lac's.

We should use his team or a team from Sweden, I have some good idea's for the beginning.

I will show you different scripts, so you get the idea, I rather like parts of Mussouri, because I know the terrain well. It could also have a few other places to give the combined effect

But the view to Nanda Devi is great from there. I could do a lot of short (3 men) crew pickup shots at Simla, Nainital, and Dhera Dun to add depth.

Warm regards to you and your family, I will call you, Bergman's actresses in Stockholm might be a key -

With "Great Exspectations"

Conrad Rooks

Extract from Review of *Plans for Departure**

The mention of revolution or religion can clear a bookshop fiction aisle faster than a fire alarm. Readers shy from such knotty themes with good reason: they can send novelists up in smoke. Norman Mailer changed his form to 'the new journalism' and his focus to himself as he tried to chronicle the 1968 US political conventions in *Miami and the Siege of Chicago*. Joseph Heller was reduced to Las Vegas one-liners in *God Knows,* his retelling of the Biblical King David story. But with a chilly wit and metaphysical calm, India's prize-winning Nayantara Sahgal has mastered the difficult task.

---

* *Time* Magazine, 23 September 1985

Letter from Earl Miner*

Prof. Earl Miner

FELLOW OF THE WOODROW WILSON INTERNATIONAL CENTER FOR SCHOLARS *Smithsonian Institution Building Washington D.C. 20560*

6 March 82

Dear Tara,

I have just finished reading Day after having read Storm, as you know. It seems to me the surest test of a novelist that there be the ability to convey how people think and feel. It has been gratifying to the point of awe to observe how thoroughly convincingly, fully, you understand how men as well as women and children work. I cannot get over the elucidation you provide how I as a man tick. Of course you have not written about me in any ordinary sense. But you certainly have written about us. What I am trying to say in my fumbling fashion is that those two novels about India are really about common humanity. That is your gift, and your gift to us.

I have some questions--and that seems to be appropriate to novels in which characters question. Do you share my sense that Day is, in some sense a satirical romance and Storm as it were a simple novel? I ask this preferring Storm while acknowledging the brilliance and range of Day.

Two more questions. The first chiefly about Storm. Is it a novel that gives us hope? The second: what is the reception of your novels in India--surely that must be of some moment to you?

On reading these novels, I felt that I understood more about India, you, and myself. Such accessions are rare and precious. So, thank you, Tara, and please respond as you will.

With my gratitude for new understanding,
and affectionate wishes,

Earl

* Prof. Earl Miner was a Fellow at the Woodrow Wilson International Center for Scholars during my own fellowship there in 1981-82.

PART THREE

Fighting the Emergency

Letter to Dr R.S. Kelkar

10 Massey Hall
Jai Singh Road
New Delhi 110 001
14 May 1976

Dr R.S. Kelkar
Secretary, Sahitya Akademi
Rabindra Bhavan
New Delhi 110001

Dear Dr Kelkar,

Thank you for your letter of 20/21 April.

I wrote to you on 27 August 1975 on the matter of censorship, and you assured me in your reply of 29 August that you would place my letter before the president of the Akademi on 8 September. You now say that you have had no time to do so.

The question of free expression and the free circulation of ideas is crucial to a free society. I should have thought nothing could be as important as this to the Sahitya Akademi, which is concerned with writers and their work. Your failure to bring this issue to the notice of the president convinces me that the Sahitya Akademi of India does not concern itself with free expression. Indeed it seems willing to be a servile body, an obedient servant of dictatorship. Let me assure you that had Jawaharlal Nehru, its founder, been alive today, he would not have tolerated such a situation. Indeed he would probably have been in jail, for he would not have kept quiet on any matter concerning human freedom.

I regret I cannot serve on any committee that is so lost to self-respect as to remain silent on the censorship that is strangulating India today. Kindly accept my resignation. I hope you will be good enough to convey the precise reason for it to the other members of the Advisory Board for English, and to place it on your records.

I am sending a copy of this letter to the president and the vice-president of the Sahitya Akademi.

Yours sincerely,
Nayantara Sahgal

A Barbarous Situation

[Excerpts from Nayantara Sahgal's letters to the Authors' Guild of India in 1975, protesting against the censorship and suspension of civil liberties. She resigned membership of the Executive Commiittee of the Guild when the guild refused to put on record a protest against checks on freedom of expression.]

Since 26 June we have an 'Emergency' in this country and the government has imposed censorship and suspended civil liberties. Tens of thousands have been imprisoned without trial. I consider this a barbarous situation. I personally cannot associate myself with any organization that seeks government patronage in these conditions much less be present at any function presided over by a member of this government. I would venture to suggest that there are issues at stake in India today that the members of the executive committee would do well to think about, particularly as to how they will concern writers in future, quite apart from how they will affect the entire country.

We are not faced with a 'political' issue in a normal political situation. We are faced with a dictatorship which has ruthlessly demonstrated its policies and intentions. No further proof is needed of any government's utter immorality and shamelessness. I think myself, the country is more important than the Authors' Guild. It is in any case absolutely vital for all thinking, educated persons to declare themselves at such a time and not to fall meekly in line with the tyranny that now rules us.

The Emergency has made it clear, if any clarity were needed, what kind of government we are dealing with in its naked disregard of democratic functioning and human rights. I feel it would be totally lacking in self-respect to seek any assistance from it, much less make a patron of it. The Western democracies you mention are democracies. They have not raped the decencies or destroyed hard-built institutions. There is simply no comparison between them and the present Government of India. I hope this situation will change but no change is brought about by a servile population and certainly not by an educated elite that falls in line with every excess a dictatorship commits. I am very certain that I can be no party to any of this.

A Letter from Mrs Gandhi's India*

On 26 June 1975, Indira Gandhi, using as an argument that the Opposition had plans to overthrow the government, declared an emergency in India and arrested an estimated 100,000 citizens during the next few months. In later speeches she and other government spokesmen also insisted that the Opposition was receiving money and help from abroad for its plans. She did not produce any evidence for her accusation, and no one accused of the monstrous charge of conspiracy has been produced in court to answer it.

According to the prime minister, the chief 'conspirator' is Jayaprakash Narayan, for whom non-violence, in the tradition of Mahatma Gandhi, is an article of faith. Jayaprakash, aged seventy-three, was released 16 November presumably because of his suddenly and dramatically deteriorating health in detention. Only the restoration of a free society in India will uncover the reason why he came so close to death in the hands of government doctors and in the care of India's two premier medical institutions, both government-owned, the All-India Institute of Medical Sciences at Delhi and the Postgraduate Medical Institute at Chandigarh. Now, cared for by private doctors in Bombay, he has made a partial recovery though the damage to his kidneys is permanent and he will

* *The New Republic,* 7 and 14 August 1976

never be normally active again. Another 'conspirator' is Morarji Desai, also an apostle of non-violence. Aged eighty-one, he is still in detention. Significantly, he has refused to eat any cooked food in jail, except what is, on occasion, provided by his family. These are perhaps the last two living Gandhian leaders of national stature now left in India. They did, it is true, wish most emphatically to replace Mrs Gandhi's government, believing that in a democratic system governments are and should be replaced when they fail to fulfil their mandate or when they transgress the limits of decent and democratic functioning.

Mrs Gandhi's government had clearly failed to fulfil the enthusiastic mandate it had received in 1971 – a disappointment Indians could have lived with had her government not also come to represent and shield growing corruption in its own ranks, and a vulgar and arrogant use of power that made a mockery of democratic procedures and the decencies of life. Her own insensitivity to the rising resentment against such behaviour and her refusal to consider specific charges brought in Parliament against ministers known to be corrupt, e.g., Bansi Lal (now defense minister) and L.N. Mishra (former railway minister, killed by a bomb explosion in early 1975), went far to aggravate conditions of severe economic distress. In 1974, a popular movement against her government took shape and a perennially divided Opposition began to come together under Jayaprakash Narayan to discuss such issues as the erosion of citizens' rights, corruption that included the manner of collection and use of money by the Congress and the need for electoral and educational reform – all of which had assumed grave national proportions. The demand that she should cleanse the Congress and take action against the corrupt began to be heard within her own party. It became obvious that there was a growing caucus within the Congress dissatisfied with her leadership, who did not believe she had a divine right to rule.

When Mrs Gandhi declared an emergency, she acted in character. Having become increasingly authoritarian over the past six years, she finally took the plunge. Three events seem to have precipitated the decision. The election in Gujarat state in early June 1975 revealed that a united opposition could get the better of the Congress. With the general election due less than a year away, this was an ominous sign. On 12 June, the Allahabad High Court judgment found her guilty of corruption on two counts in the conduct of her election to Parliament in 1971. The judge's courage caused a stir; his judgment did not. Her ambiguous and evasive statements in court, reported in detail in the newspapers, had left the public with the definite impression that she had been neither straightforward nor truthful. Her agent, Yashpal Kapoor, a highly controversial political figure, had made matters worse for her by his own brash statements in court. But above all, her own party seemed to be coming to the boil, alerting her to a possible move to replace her. Among those spearheading a dialogue with Jayaprakash Narayan and Opposition parties were the brilliant young radicals, Chandrashekhar, Mohan Dharia and Krishna Kant, who had in 1969 helped to engineer a split in' the Congress, outwit the Old Guard and raise her to unrivalled leadership. Their brains, influence and backing could not be underestimated. After the Allahabad judgment, a group of Congressmen openly urged her to step down pending the Supreme Court's decision on her appeal, in the interests of democratic functioning. When it became clear to her that she would not be allowed to appoint a substitute of her own choice to take her place, who would fade out in her favour later, she realized she was in real danger of not getting her position back.

The emergency paid immediate dividends. A sweep of arrests in the night had the advantage of surprise attack. Censorship immobilized the press. It also covered the country with an unnatural blanket of silence, for nobody knew what was going on. Criticism, oral or written, of the government, was forbidden. More than five people could not congregate without special permission. Permission was freely given to 'spontaneous demonstrations' in support of the prime minister. And the flash and flourish of naked power left her party in no doubt about how far the leader was willing to go to keep herself in the saddle. Those still out of jail who had shown signs of rebellion had second thoughts. Armed guards were put on duty on the houses of cabinet ministers, ostensibly for their protection.

Once it was launched, the dictatorship was easy to perpetuate. The last few years had prepared the ground, providing her with a 'committed' civil service which understood that it would not be tolerated unless obedience and loyalty to the prime minister were its first concerns; a police force built up to match the army in numbers, and in sophisticated weaponry and intelligence devices; a system of surveillance by which she kept her ministers and party members in line by the dossiers in her possession. Few of these instruments, except police control, were necessary in the countryside where the people were largely unlettered. But they were necessary in the cities.

Delegations of traders, teachers, students, workers, writers, businessmen and trade unionists were ordered to appear at her residence to congratulate her on the emergency and offer support to her 'Twenty-Point Programme.' Huge posters hailing her leadership, along with pictures of her in every shop window, burgeoned overnight. Anxious to overcome the charge, in her own party and the general public, of the communist influence on her, she put a deliberate distance between herself and the Moscow-directed Communist Party of India, her chief ally. She could afford to do so as she had Moscow's unqualified support. The CPI was obliged to go along with her, whatever its private thoughts about her new moves. These were headed by putting her much advertised 'radicalism' into cold storage with concessions to industry, the withdrawal of a fixed bonus to workers her government had announced three years earlier and a budget that cheered and mollified the rich. Her son, Sanjay, who had failed to produce an indigenous car for which he had been granted an exclusive government licence in 1970, generous support from industrial backers and 290 acres of requisitioned land – and whose failure had become one of the now buried scandals of her regime

– was projected as a 'youth leader' and pragmatist, proof that the Congress was not committed to any particular ideology, only to progress. Sanjay was also projected as Mrs Gandhi's political heir, setting the dynastic seal on her dictatorial coup and setting at rest any speculation about who would succeed her. The Congress has thus been reduced to Mrs Gandhi's personal possession to pass on, and India a classic example of Asian dictatorship.

In these circumstances, the question often put to her, of when she plans to lift the Emergency, has become irrelevant, for lifting it will make little difference to India. Mrs Gandhi has used her opportunity since 26 June last year to end all legitimate and constitutional challenge to her personal rule and to cripple the institutions through which that challenge could come. This has been done under constitutional cover. Parliament met from 21 July to 7 August 1975 to crucially amend the Constitution and sanction – as the law of the land – the violations of civil liberties. Some thirty MPs were in jail – Opposition leaders (except those of the CPI) and those belonging to her own party who she feared were going to lead a confrontation against her.

The censors in New Delhi and the state capitals whose job it is to black out news and opinions inconvenient to the government – and they cover the whole territory of newspapers, magazines, commentary, fiction, theatre and films – may be dispensed with once the Emergency is lifted, but control of all media will continue. Radio and television are a government monopoly in any case, and in the past Mrs Gandhi has used them blatantly to promote herself and her party and distort happenings in India. Now a single news agency, Samachar, feeds the press with official handouts. Respected editors have been thrown out of their jobs and replaced by sycophants, and newspaper management, already government-manipulated, will soon be its complete tool in what the minister for information and broadcasting picturesquely describes as 'restructuring the entire newspaper industry so as to make it accountable to the people'. In today's official jargon this means government's iron hand. This week two of the last dissident voices were silenced. A one-man weekly, *Opinion,* was simply shut down; a tiny-circulation monthly read mostly by intellectuals, *Seminar,* put itself out of business rather than submit its pages to the censors. The power of the censors is reflected in the fact that, as of this writing, not one of the supine Indian press has reported the untimely death of these periodicals.

A new law was passed last August making election disputes relating to the president, the vice-president, prime minister and speaker non-justiciable. And the Representation of the People Act was amended retrospectively in order to legalize the very issues on which the prime minister had been indicted in her election case – an extraordinarily brazen piece of legislation since her case was already pending in the Supreme Court. Thus any genuine judgment by the court was nullified in advance. With no legal scope left to operate in, it was obliged to exonerate her. The lesson of those who rebel foreclosed other options.

Even if the Emergency is lifted, Opposition parties will take long to recover from the bludgeoning authoritarian rule has given them. Thousands of their political workers are in jail and a relentless campaign to discredit them as enemies of the people is carried on by the government in circumstances where they are not free to answer charges or be reported in the press. They would find themselves severely damaged in human resources and in funds if an election were announced, and without the full restoration of press freedom and civil liberties there can be no free and fair election. No one expects one either.

After the political opposition, Mrs Gandhi's main target has been the universities. Delhi and Jawaharlal Nehru Universities, both in the capital and among the country's most prestigious institutions, have been subjected to searches and arrests. At one time, soon after the Emergency was proclaimed, nearly the whole Sanskrit department of Delhi University was in jail, a warning to those who had Jan Sang (Right) affiliations or sympathies. But followers of the Communist Party of India (Marxist), which is bitterly opposed to the regime, have not fared much better. People with a living to earn and families to feed will think twice before openly dissenting.

Lifting the Emergency will leave intact the vast police force, as big as the army and inflated with powers. Law and order is a state subject but the Border Security Force, used for defence, is far better armed than the normal police force, and has been freely used along with the powerful Central Reserve Police Force against citizens. The government showed its police might and muscle when it arbitrarily dismissed Tamil Nadu's Opposition government on 31 January, instead of holding the state election due at the time, or postponing it for the duration of the Emergency as the general election has been postponed.

Censorship has been the most highly effective instrument of India's dictatorship, keeping people ignorant about an event in another town or even half a mile away in their own town. The enormity of censorship, we now know, can never be understood by people in countries where information is freely available, where there is a continuous flow of news, and where views of all kinds can be freely expressed. Indians today are in ignorance about what is happening in India and only those world events reach them that the censors pass as suitable for consumption. Very few people heard about the non-violent protest begun in Delhi and four states (UP, Bihar, Maharashtra and Andhra Pradesh) on 14 November, Jawaharlal Nehru's birthday, and concluded on 26 January. Republic Day, though it daily offered up batches of peaceful protectors to the police and was led by citizens as eminent as Maniben Patel, Sardar Patel's daughter. Several jailbreaks, major news items in ordinary times, were not permitted to be reported at all. News about them travelled by grapevine. But one has learned to read between the lines of newspaper accounts. This does not take much ingenuity since our leaders have become drearily repetitive and the current jargon they use provides definite clues to their statements. Reference to 'rightist fascist forces regrouping' means the Opposition is refusing to surrender or be wiped out. One positive result of the Emergency, in fact, has been to bring a divided Opposition closer together and to blur the barriers between left, right and centre. As in British times, the issue is freedom. When senior officials meet in Delhi to discuss stricter security measures along with the transfer and dismissal of jail staff and officers, the perceptive reader realizes the jailbreak accounts he has heard must be substantially true.

In April, the family planning drive, an objective with which there is widespread agreement among the educated, made inadvertent news when bungling and bullying tactics misfired, leading to an angry demonstration at Turkman Gate, a predominantly Muslim locality in Old Delhi. This was not, of course, reported in the newspapers, though the crowd turned violent, leading to a riot, with thirty or more people killed and hundreds arrested. But the news was too explosive to be contained and word of it spread fast. Earlier the Delhi administration had announced that anyone expecting a third child would not get a ration card; government-employed teachers would have to get five people sterilized if they wanted to keep their jobs; no one due a government house allotment would get it till he produced a sterilization certificate; and vans had rounded up young and old, married and unmarried for 'the operation'. The fury at Turkman Gate had been in response to forcible evictions of its inhabitants from the area along with the administration's family planning methods. That there must be some truth in the news of deaths and arrests on a considerable scale became evident when about a week after the event an array of spokesmen swung into identical explanation like an orchestra with everybody playing the violin. The lieutenant governor of Delhi denied that people were being forcibly sterilized. The health minister hastened to make it clear in Parliament that the union government 'was not for pressure or harassment in implementing the programme' and was ruling out compulsory sterilization for the parents of more than two children. A team of reporters sent to 'investigate allegations of forcible sterilization' found them 'entirely false'. And a government release stated in predictable language that 'certain unsocial and frustrated elements were circulating rumours that rations would not be issued nor salaries paid to persons not undergoing sterilization'. It warned the people to be on guard against 'such anti-national and antisocial elements and their nefarious designs'. None of this vehement denial explained why the new family planning centre set up with much fanfare at Dojana House, Old Delhi, had abruptly been shut down, nor the flood of resentment that continued to fill the air. But this unceremonious retreat on an issue where the Catholics had already expressed firm disapproval, and the Muslims had flared into actual violence, is an interesting aspect of manoeuvre required even in a dictatorship. Modifying Delhi's rough sterilization drive is probably based on an assessment that the subject is inflammable and the Muslims must be handled with care. But in our irrational political situation it could simply be based on the possibility of a third expected child for Mrs Gandhi's elder son. In any event it would be a tragedy if the campaign is not soon converted to education and effective remedy, for on this issue, Emergency or no Emergency, we cannot afford to fail.

Introduction to *A Voice for Freedom**

I had lived in Delhi nearly two years and written for newspapers on a variety of subjects when the Congress split in 1969 riveted my attention to the political scene. Something different had struck it with the impact of a blast. This was not a parting of the ways based on genuine differences of opinion and programme. This was an emotional bid for personal power. It made a carnival of principle, procedure and convention – dull words, of no use at all for street arousal – and went on to make a carnival of politics and economics.

By 1971 it was clear to me that Indians were being pushed towards an authoritarian order. The country would be slipped into it if possible, and bludgeoned into it if necessary. One significant sign of this was the condition of the Congress itself. It was being deprived of discussion and debate. Its rungs of command were being cut away. The good leadership material within it was being held in check, and later dispensed with, while obliging mediocrity was brought forward and put in key positions. A party that ignores its own constitution, and stifles its own democratic processes and available talent, is obviously not committed to or concerned with democracy in the country or a free society as a value. A ruling oligarchy was emerging, some of whose leading lights were transferees from the CPI.

---

* Published by Hind Pocket Books, 1977

No propaganda effort was spared to set up the one-party one-leader idea. Eventually, the Emergency gave its seal and sanction to this development in a series of steps. Mrs Gandhi had the law changed to immunize herself – a leader above the law – against the Allahabad High Court judgment. Congress President Barooah informed his party and the public that India was Indira and Indira was India – and no one contradicted him. A proposal was circulated, and later withdrawn and disowned by the government, advocating a 'presidential form' of government for India, headed by a president armed with considerable personal powers. And finally, in 1976, came the amendment package in Parliament that made the prime minister a virtual dictator. In a nation reduced to silence, even dynastic succession could be unabashedly promoted. But these trends in the making were visible much earlier than the Emergency, and it needed no special insight, only an observation of events, personalities and atmosphere to recognize them.

To my surprise not many who should have, did. In Delhi the breed known as 'intellectual' seemed happy to repeat the current 'socio-economic' jargon and to believe we had entered an era of real change. Disagreement with those at the top was apt to earn one the label of 'reactionary', and certainly the cold shoulder as far as recognition and opportunities went. I remember feeling a tremendous relief when in December 1973 Jayaprakash Narayan issued an alert in the form of a letter to members of Parliament, and one to youth, urging ways and means of protecting our civic freedoms and democratic institutions and setting up Citizens for Democracy for this purpose.

The Bihar movement grew out of this and related needs the following year, and became a massive, organized, peaceful protest, first against the ineffective Bihar government, and later against the union government's refusal to listen to just demands. Its popularity and the success of its demonstrations, due in part to the cooperation of sections of the Opposition, gave the Opposition its first platform for national unity, and this had an immediate effect on its performance in Parliament and state assemblies, on by-elections, and finally in the Gujarat state election in June 1975. It confronted the Congress with the first serious political challenge it had faced since Independence. Combined with the Congress party's own opportunity to replace Mrs Gandhi after the Allahabad High Court judgment, it resulted in Mrs Gandhi declaring the Emergency.

As a political writer for the *Indian Express* I had been a critic of what I saw as the main current since 1969, a muddled 'radicalism' masking the growth and entrenchment of personal rule, unaccountable, it seemed, to any forum. So I had been an outcast with the Establishment for several years before I became interested and involved in JP's experiment in Bihar and a columnist for his weekly, *Everyman's* in September 1974. By that time the Establishment looked upon me with grave suspicion, even as something of an aberration as a member of 'the family' who did not seek patronage or make obeisance, and who refused to be squeezed into line.

It will illustrate the mood in the capital when I say that the more timid among my acquaintances in and outside official circles stopped coming to my house at this time. A friend of many years in the Indian Foreign Service confessed it would be awkward for him to do so. A journalist doing extremely well under government patronage, who had once solicited my articles for her page, found herself unwell or otherwise occupied on the two occasions I invited her to meet friends at my apartment. I was, in fact, surrounded by signs of disapproval. A relation of mine remarked that on a trip to Bihar I had wandered around with goondas, not a very accurate description of two young activists of the Bihar movement in whose company I had visited Arrah. The Supreme Court lawyer who accosted me (there is no other word for it) at a dinner party in Delhi to inform me I was 'marching out of step' and told me to change the tone of my articles as well as the newspaper I regularly wrote for is another example of the lack of mind or manners with which power so often infects those on the comfortable side of it. In Calcutta on a visit in early 1975, my sister said that Chief Minister Siddhartha Shankar Ray had told her with a mixture of seriousness and humour, in reference to my newspaper writings: 'We could pick her up under MISA any day.'

There were signs too that the ardour with which I had been wooed as a writer was fast fading. A lecturer in English at Delhi University, commissioned by the American publisher Twayne, to write a critique of my work, and who had taken material from me for his project about three years earlier, simply vanished from my acquaintance. A film-maker, enthusiastic about filming my novel *This Time of Morning*, abandoned the idea after obtaining funds from abroad and deciding on the film stars who would play the leading roles. She said by way of apology that the book was too difficult to film and she hoped I would write something with fewer characters – though the characters in the book had not grown in number since she had read it. I came to the conclusion that the lecturer found it politic not to connect himself with me. And the film-maker, who lived abroad at the time, probably discovered during her two-year wait for funds that I was too outspokenly opposed to the government to risk her own acceptability with the ruling clique. The areas of television, information and broadcasting – her special concerns – needed government's direct sanction for programmes.

Such indications, while they were profoundly disturbing as evidence of the narrow, rigid atmosphere about us, and the kind of either-or line-up it demanded, also served as excellent material for writing, and I put it to good use. Two novels, *The Day in Shadow* and *A Situation in New Delhi*, reflected the mounting unease and at times the feeling of impending disaster I had as I wrote them.

The time served me well too because it put me in touch with men and women in the Opposition. It seemed to me there was far more going on there both in idealism and practical thinking than in the now servile ranks of the Congress. Opposition talent came from the professions, the trade unions, the universities and the countryside, from the Right, Left and Centre. I was impressed by the spectacle in Bihar, of an organized, disciplined youth movement, committed to non-violence and change. Their meetings and activities were more stirring than anything I had seen in twenty-five years. The more I saw of all this, the more absurd and dangerous the Delhi delusion of a one-party one-leader system looked. Some obliging entrepreneur had by now put up a huge poster proclaiming this idea in Connaught Place. It gave me a shiver down my spine each time I passed it.

When the Emergency came, like a numbing blow in the dark, the manner of it was shocking though the word 'dictatorship' was common usage by then. After Mujibur Rehman's establishment of a dictatorship in Bangladesh in early 1975, many in India waited for it as we wait for the monsoon, knowing that, sooner or later, it is coming. JP warned a public meeting of the possibility. But no one realized how soon or suddenly it would come, and how well-executed it would be. Suddenly we inhabited a police state. Unknown tens of thousands were in jail and it was not fashionable to ask the reason why. Cliches bounced off the tongues of the only people permitted to speak – spokesmen of the Congress, the CPI, and those who supported the Emergency.

There were times when I could have put my head in my hands and wept that a nation accustomed to Jawaharlal Nehru's heart-searching and eloquence, a party once led by towering intellects, should now be at the mercy of a handful of mini-brains with three-and-a-half catch phrases between them in place of a vocabulary. Dictatorship, it was obvious, apart from its brutalities, was going to be excruciatingly boring. When 'anti-fascist' conferences began to be held – with blood-and-thunder language used to describe these invisible (and as far as I could tell, non-existent) enemies of the people – Emergency language reached its peak of inanity. At the request of a lawyer friend in the Socialist Party I wrote a pamphlet for underground distribution, particularly at Patna, where the government was to hold a World Anti-Fascist Conference in

December 1975. I quoted Nehru's speeches and writings to define fascism, and to point out that the definition squarely fitted the government in power. The pamphlet, I am told, flourished. Above ground my writing did not fare so well.

Everyman's had been shut down at the declaration of Emergency and Ajit Bhattacharjea, its editor, told me the police had shredded the last issue – an extraordinarily vindictive gesture, but in keeping with the fascist techniques used to intimidate all opposition. (Ajit had saved a copy of the last issues and I promptly and lovingly laid all my issues of *Everyman's* to rest in a safe place until they could surface again.) I could still write for the *Indian Express,* Editor-in-Chief S. Mulgaokar told me, but not on any political subject. He was waiting himself to be told to leave and had stayed on this long only to help the owners over a difficult period.

I thought hard about a subject and came up with abortion. It is an important subject, of course, and I had once been summoned by a parliamentary committee to offer my views on it when legislation was being considered. But having contributed what understanding I could to the subject I had to think hard again about what to write next. One of the Shukla brothers had remarked with ill-concealed satisfaction to my mother at a wedding lunch we had all attended that now Nayantara would not be able to write about politics. My mother had retorted with her accustomed vigour that politics was not the only subject in the world, that civilized people had much else to talk and write about, and that her daughter, who was a novelist, had no dearth of topics to comment on. I tried to live up to this compliment and to be creative, but a ban on any side of creativity is a ban on all of it.

There is an indignity in being told virtually to shut up, which self-respecting people, especially those whose profession it is to think and write, find hard to accept. I kept thinking too of the various ironies in this situation. My father Ranjit Sitaram Pandit, a Sanskrit scholar, a lover of languages, learning and literature, had cut these and much else that was dear to him out of his life when he joined the national movement, involving himself with politics and jail, because he had believed, like so many of his compatriots, that freedom came first. He had also believed his sacrifice would make it possible for future scholars and artists to do the work they loved best, unharassed and in freedom.

My uncle Jawaharlal Nehru, a writer himself, had felt particularly tender towards the breed and had remained unshakable in his pledge that whatever Indians lacked, they would not lack freedom of expression; that there was no double standard of values – one for rich countries and another for the poor. There were some things that were the breath of life, and everyone needed them. I wondered what he would have thought of the Sahitya Akademi he had founded, unwilling now to utter even a sigh in protest. But I had a living to earn and I had to come up with a subject interesting enough for readers and innocuous enough for the censor. Reader interest was an even more important consideration now that reading matter had become so dreary, and the speeches and public utterances we heard so repetitive. If one did not die of boredom, one might well go mad just listening to the sameness.

Newspapers had become a drag for it was news, above all, that was not available. One newspaper was too many to read when I had always read four. I wondered if the censor would object to adultery as a topic. Apparently, he did not, and my next article was 'Adultery in Life and Literature'. It provoked Acharya Kripalani to the typical humourous retort in the press that he wished, he like Nayantara, could combat the woes of censorship through literary outlets of this sort. I did not see this remark when it was published, but he repeated it to me when we met in the corridors of the All-India Institute of Medical Sciences during JP's halt there in November 1975 on his way to hospital in Bombay. A knot of us, standing disconsolately about, were even able to laugh a little, and we needed to laugh in those days.

But soon my need to write what needed to be written was so overwhelming that my next two articles dealt with dissent in other times and the atrocious punishments dealt out to those who had disobeyed authority. I recalled that one could be sentenced to death by poison for teaching the values of the good life, if these were different from what the state taught. One could be burned at the stake, broken on the wheel or condemned to the galleys for declaring, writing or printing 'heresies' against the Church or the monarch, or challenging current theories about the sun, the earth and the stars. From Socrates to Servetus and beyond, prison torture or extermination had been ordinary, matter-of-fact punishments for those who disagreed.

India was now adding a new chapter of her own to the record. I could not say so in so many words, but that was the inference – for I had a mounting horror of the Gulag Archipelago growing invisibly about us – the unnamed, unnumbered, unreported, undefended arrests, all the faceless multitude behind bars, in jails becoming monstrously overcrowded in the sweltering July–August–September heat of India. For the few who could eventually, after much hardship, heartbreak, expense and red tape, be visited by their next of kin, there were thousands who could not. We do not know what these people suffered – the 'average' citizen who was now the 'average' prisoner – and how many of them fell ill, despaired or died. If people like himself, writers, journalists and other obstinate nuisances were intended to be in their number, the plan was obviously abandoned – though the threat continued – after Kuldip Nayar's arrest, which gave the regime a bad name and adverse publicity abroad.

Our tribe was, in any case, immobilized by censorship. Knowing my inability to stay immobilized very long, a Muslim friend, whom I seldom saw as he was very much a pillar of the Establishment, took the trouble to toil up the two flights of stairs to my apartment in the furnace heat, to warn me to 'lie low' as my comings and goings were watched and my telephone tapped. (Or did he say bugged? Anyway, the telephone was watching me too.) I knew there was something odd going on, because on three occasions when I made a complaint about its functioning, the whole instrument was removed and changed. My friend said the awesome fact of power had to be recognized. The power set-up was here to stay. The sooner one bowed to it, the better. All resistance, he said, had been wiped out. It was no use hoping for a change.

Part of this was, no doubt, true. An American correspondent who had visited Bihar had told me that all traces of the Bihar movement had been crushed like a cigarette butt under a boot, and by way of demonstration he had graphically ground his own heel into the carpet. But I knew that all resistance had not been wiped out. It never had, in any century, in any part of the world, under any sort of regime. The police state around us was evidence that it had not here. And if history teaches us anything, it is that power is never here to stay. I told my friend so and we had a futile quarrel, leaving us both angry and shaken. He departed on his well-intentioned round to warn others to 'lie low',' while I wondered how much damage he would succeed in doing by creating fear and bruising morale.

Earning a living was becoming more of a problem. Having commented obliquely on our 'Gulag Archipelago' I could not think of one more thing to say for the newspapers. And my novel writing, which my mother had believed would save me from oblivion, presented its own difficulties. Now it was not a question of what was written, but who had written it. Dr Lakshmi Narayan Lal, JP's Hindi biographer, who had discussed with me a Hindi translation by him of *The Day in Shadow,* told me the Hindi publisher found it unwise to produce my book at the present time. One publisher who had contracted to publish *A Situation in New Delhi,* apologized for not being able to do so and withdrew their contract. (If a contract is broken or nullified by circumstances beyond normal control – an act of God or state – I suppose there is nothing an author can do about it. I concluded that the overnight appearance of a dictatorship was such an act.) Another publisher, eager to pick up the option, also found it unsafe to handle, on the informal advice, they said, of someone in the censor's office.

Fiction often foreshadows fact. *The Day in Shadow* had had as an accompanying backdrop to Simrit's divorce settlement, the growing Soviet influence on our subcontinent and a definite Indian tilt in that direction. I finished writing the book in February 1971. The Indo-Soviet Treaty, a landmark of its kind, embodying this tilt, was not signed until August that year. The 'situation' creeping upon us in *A Situation in New Delhi* – a book I had completed writing in January 1975 – was upon us in June, and I myself was hung with it.

I went to see the chief censor. Harry D'Penha had been called out of retirement to handle this vital lever of dictatorship. He was cheerful and welcoming. In the past I had received the most courteous assistance from him when I had had occasion to seek special information. Harry advised me to wait till things eased up, if I had any doubts about my material. He also said the home ministry, not his department, handled books. He also expressed surprise that I should need advice about publishing. What could I have written that could not be published? Apparently there was one person in the land – and he, the chief censor – who did not know how the Establishment felt about me and how unacceptable my name and views were. Of course I did not go to the home ministry. There would have been no point unless I had changed my name on the manuscript to Susie Brown. I took my manuscript home and forgot about it. It had no importance now next to the sheer sickness I felt when I thought of admired, veteran leaders – some legendary for their contribution to India – in jail, of the many thousands with no famous name or background to protect them.

I had received from the P.E.N. in Bombay its resolution condemning censorship and had written to Madame Sophia Wadia congratulating the organization. It was the very least, I thought, that a writers' body could do. The previous year I had been invited to become a member of the Executive Committee of the newly set up Authors' Guild of India, and had accepted. It seemed a worthwhile cause if it could help struggling authors with their publishing and other problems. I found, actually, that my presence on the committee, as indeed that of the other members, was superfluous. Justice G.D. Khosla, president, and D.R. Mankekar, general secretary, conducted meetings between them with a very perfunctory attention to the others present. Both gentlemen were publicity-minded and, I felt, extremely anxious to be favourites at court. The plans they had for the Guild, it seemed to me, were heavily and needlessly dependent on the government for favour, funds and patronage. The presence, at the opening conference of the Guild, of the prime minister, if possible, or another minister, if necessary, was taken for granted. While this point appeared irrelevant to me in 1974, it appalled me in 1975. Representatives of a regime that stacked people into jail like last year's logs of firewood had no business, as far as I was concerned, on any respectable platform. I waited for some sign that the Guild would protest, not only against censorship, crippling to all real writing, but against imprisonment without trial, and would take up the cause of writers in prison.

Not a word was said about this, while a conference was busily planned for December with a cabinet minister presiding. I recommended we pass a resolution of the sort the P.E.N. had passed and gave Mr Mankekar a copy. I got no answer. The meeting went on as if nothing had happened. I thought the P.E.N. resolution, slipped into the general secretary's file, would be taken up at a later meeting. It was not. Neither the president nor the secretary made mention of it. I was deeply shocked by this attitude on the part of two men who profess to be concerned with human values. I resigned from the Guild's Executive Committee, succinctly stating my reasons in a correspondence with Mr Mankekar. As I believed my resignation was not brought to the notice of the other members of the committee promptly, I put an advertisement in the *Indian Express* to this effect. In a dictatorship situation it is important, to my mind, to be publicly clear-cut about one's beliefs if possible. For many people, whose dependents may suffer thereby, this is not possible. There were times, and this was one of them, when I felt I acted for those who wished to speak but could not. I was happy to note that a Guild member, Wing Commander S.N. Rampal, carried on a battle of his own with the Executive Committee about its conduct of Guild affairs, including the fact that my resignation and the reasons for it had not been put before the Guild. I had occasion to resign from the Sahitya Akademi's Advisory Board for English for the same reasons a few months later, in May 1976. I was asked not to press my resignation until the Akademi's Executive Board met to consider it. The meeting finally took place, I believe, in September 1976, when my resignation was accepted. This august body saw no reason either, it appears, to raise its voice on behalf of freedom.

I looked around at the debris of the vigourous, independent penmanship of which India had been justly proud. Respected editors and journalists were out of jobs, or making do with what they could find. Sycophancy had grown to fantastic proportions. I had already stopped my subscription to the *Hindustan Times* and the *Illustrated Weekly of India*, some of whose classic issues will, I hope, be preserved as museum pieces. Meeting friends was something of a relief, but even a social gathering was distressing when 'walls had ears' and conversation had to be guarded.

Yet parties were the only source of stray fragments of real news, and one clung to the fragments one got. Sometimes parties became strained and tense too. At the home of a friend I had a fierce argument with a Congress member of parliament, whose argument suddenly collapsed with the pathetic statement that it would take the next generation trained in subversion and firearms, to overthrow the present set-up in the Congress and the country. It struck me that an MP who could in desperation speak this way of his party and the condition it had brought about, yet with no will to act against it, did indeed belong to its last gasp. And I was more convinced than ever that the shadow of defeat lay over the Congress, and the power structure, ostensibly invulnerable, was hollow within. But things might go on this way for months and years, a waste of time that could be spent usefully somewhere else. And I gratefully accepted an opportunity to go to the United States on a six-month research scholarship at the Radcliffe Institute. I remained abroad until August 1977, writing and teaching, first in Cambridge, Massachusetts, where I worked on a book, and later at Southern Methodist University in Dallas, Texas, where as writer-in-residence I led two seminars on creative writing. My stay abroad gave me the opportunity to try to acquaint Americans with events in India. The contents of this book (*A Voice for Freedom*), except for an article I wrote for the *Times* (London), are the result of my endeavours.

I acknowledged authorship of an article I wrote for the *New Republic* under the pseudonym Azad when Leila Fernandes, in exile with her son, and tormented with anxiety about her husband, asked me if she could use my name in her statement in Washington before a committee of Congress for international relations. The Indian embassy in Washington sent a senior diplomat, Mr Inam Rahman, to my seminar at the Radcliffe Institute in November 1976, and a month later Mr Janaki Butt of the Indian consulate general in New York attended my talk at Columbia University. Neither attempted conversation with me. I suppose you do not chat pleasantly with a thorn in your side.

My activities were reported home, but they could have carried no surprises for New Delhi. Officialdom would perhaps have found it more instructive to attend an evening gathering at the home of my valued friend, longtime friend of India, and a staunch supporter of all good human causes, Dorothy Norman. I had, with her permission, invited Subramaniam Swamy, on the run from the Indian authorities at the time. After somewhat conventional talks providing the background and meaning of the Emergency by Rajni Kothari, Ved Mehta and myself, Swamy's down-to-earth remarks, crisply delivered with no ifs, buts or frills, had a tonic effect on the audience representing important human rights organizations, the P.E.N. and distinguished academics, journalists and others interested in Indian developments. The last things that many present expected of a Jan Sang leader was that he would be a modern, articulate, Harvard-educated economist, with a practical knowledge of the Indian countryside and a lively sense of humour.

'People need to know,' I told Swamy afterward, 'that the Jan Sang does not have three horns and a tail.' What I meant was that it was time people took another look at India. Three months later, after the March election, they did.

Letter from S. Mulgaonkar

THE INDIAN EXPRESS

Phone : 273951 (5 lines) Gram : Pressnews Telex : 208 - 503

Express Building, Bahadur Shah Zafar Marg, New Delhi - 1.

Mrs. Nayantara Sahgal
English Department
Southern Methodist University
Dallas, Texas 75275
U.S.A.

Dear Tara,

What a delight to hear from you. You should have been here for the end of the long night.* It was at once an exhilarating and shaming experience - the common people had given us back what we the so-called intellectuals had failed to safeguard and to fight for.

On the whole, things are shaping in an encouraging manner though I get the feeling that policy thinking will not get the attention it needs until the mess left behind by Mrs. G. is cleared.

I know how you must feel being away at a time like this. I look forward to your return to resume your writing for us. Anything you can think of doing ~~for us~~ in the meanwhile will be welcome. Why not a couple of articles on what you have already worked on- Mrs. G.'s political style

Warm regards to both of you in which Krishna joins me.

Affectionately yours

(S. Mulgaokar)

---

* The end of the Emergency

PART FOUR

My Homage to Three Greats

Intellectual Giant of the Century*

There are men who one forgets are mortal, who arouse our anger when they die, whose contribution to the world is so many-sided, increasing so phenomenally in its sweep and scope as time goes on, that they have no business to die. We do not accept their death.

Bertrand Russell was the great result, perhaps the greatest in his own long lifetime, of what a civilization in which free speculation is possible can produce. Civilization has a long history and many shades of meaning, but there is one attribute without which it cannot be so called: that is the climate which makes possible the life of the mind. There have been remarkable intellects, but few in any age like Russell's, which refused to be awed by anything under the sun.

When a mind of this dimension is involved with the suffering and savagery of its times and joins battle with them, the result is something titanic, almost beyond human proportion. Russell's life assumed this stature in his later years when he fought with all the knowledge and persuasion in his possession to warn mankind that nuclear destruction was no vague distant threat but a present, actual terror. Yet pacifist was a singular misnomer for the unrelenting war he waged on so many fronts against the lack or the miscarriage of justice. And to call him a mathematician or a philosopher was

---

* *The Sunday Standard,* 15 February 1970

never enough. What Russell gave the world was more than original thinking in mathematics and philosophy. He provided us with the astonishing and poignant spectacle over the space of nearly a century of a man who strove with his whole being to overcome in his personal relationships the painful barriers of personality, and at the public level perpetually to restate and re-enforce his links with humanity. What man strove for, he said, was 'some kind of struggling emergence of mind' – the slow and steady additional achievement that is every generation's legacy to the next and which is the journey we call civilization.

In his own career there were two aspects to this human advance. One was the pursuit of pure knowledge, and he delved deep into his own branches of knowledge in search of exactitude and truth. The other was that, if thought is man's highest achievement, then it must enter the arena to deal with practical problems. He poured the results of his own thinking on many subjects – philosophical, scientific, political, educational and moral – into more than fifty publications, in lucid, impeccable prose that any man who reads and thinks can enjoy, and became known through these to millions the world over whom pure science and philosophy neither reach nor touch. Philosophy he once defined as teaching man 'how to live without certainty and yet without being paralysed by hesitation'. There was no better example than his own life, for he plunged into active demonstration of what he stood for whenever he could, as in the case of the school he and his wife Dora started because they found established education unsatisfactory; and his participation, even at the age of ninety, in public protests against the Vietnam War and nuclear weapons. He was in this respect what few men have been, a carrier of culture, who put his ideas to work in an impressive variety of programmes and issues. From his own personal development to a deep involvement with other people's pain, there was not one flagging moment when his reliance on reason or his convictions failed him. And to the end, in spite of his disappointment and disillusionment with the progress of his fight for nuclear disarmament, he believed in the possibility of a golden age, provided man would make up his mind to choose life, not death.

There was almost no established belief he did not question. A member of the aristocracy, he gave up his inheritance. Born and educated during the Victorian era he was nevertheless, as a result of his unorthodox upbringing, nonconformist to the marrow, beginning with his surprise at the age of eleven on discovering that Euclid's geometrical axioms had to be accepted without proof, and going on to his espousal of the free trade movement, women's suffrage, his conscientious objection during the First World War, and causes as far-flung as India's independence, the truth about President Kennedy's assassination and the treatment of Jews in Soviet Russia. He expressed himself bluntly on nearly every important issue of his day and made history because he practised what he believed, from his undaunted search for the honest and loving relationship in marriage to his strenuous commitment to peace – based on so startling a concept as the utter unimportance of nationhood and national prestige as compared with the survival of the human species and its total achievement. Perhaps no scientist and no philosopher ever had as much to do with life and the living.

Russell was too big for his times, too undivided an integrity for the comfort of any Establishment, not to become the target of all kinds of attack, personal and political. He refused to follow any dictate but that of scientific intelligence. Morality for him began with that. He endured imprisonment and ridicule in his own country and vituperation in the United States. There is hardly anything so extraordinary as the witch-hunt to which America subjected him because of his views, until the McCarthy witch-hunt against Americans began. Through it all his career went on inexorably as the ocean, with something of the ocean's grandeur. His autobiography written in beautiful, often moving, language reveals a life fully and closely examined, showing the naked progress of his searches and what they meant to him.

I wonder if this is still the kind of world that can produce men like Russell. It is, first of all, increasingly the world of the specialist, in which knowledge is narrowed down more and more, almost shutting out the larger vision. It is also the world of the technician, the man with the know-how, the formula rather than the field from which it springs. The specialist and the technician, brilliant in their own departments, are apt to be lost outside these.

Then, in the last forty years or so there has been a definite authoritarian trend over a large part of the world: the communist revolution with its capture of Central Europe and China, dictators in Italy and Germany, and the dictatorships that still flourish in Spain, Portugal and many parts of Latin America. These are, or have been, areas where the exercise of personality and free speculation are not possible. Where the state or the leader is God, there are distinct limits to how far and in what direction man may go. The mind of man in vast areas has thus never operated under so many confines as it does in this century we think of as progressive. This is quite a sobering thought. And there seems to be no possibility in the foreseeable future of this picture changing.

It was once believed that the 'thaw' in the Soviet Union would produce a springtime which would set free the mind, now that the basic needs of the people – food, shelter, education – had been supplied through untold hardship and sacrifice, and world power status achieved. But that is not so. The Czechoslovak crisis proved it was not so. Events in the Soviet Union itself, with the periodic rounding up of dissenters, confirms it. We have to come to the conclusion that there is no link, no possible connection between authoritarianism and freedom. The one has to be destroyed in order to achieve the other. Neither can grow in the normal course out of the other. It is hard to see, therefore, how the spirit of man can grow wings and soar in climes such as these, deadening in the extreme.

There is also very much with us the poverty and struggle of non- communist Asia where basic needs are yet to be supplied, and which may in this decade tilt in an increasingly authoritarian direction to find its answers. If this happens there will be less and less scope for individual development. Even today we in India, with our freedoms still intact, are caught in traps from which we find it difficult to escape, chiefly the huge and growing population whose needs no successes in field and factory can cope with. Above all, can education have any meaning in this situation of swelling numbers, poorly paid teachers, ill-prepared students concerned about their future livelihood? Where, in all this, is there the possibility of training the mind, encouraging the growth of ideas? In fact, if we try to discover what India gave to civilization we have to go back to 500 BC It is a question mark whether we will, in fact, be able by some miracle to get through the next decades peacefully and in freedom. Until that happens we will have only the ghosts of such men as Russell among us, voices from the past to remind us that where men are at liberty to think there is hardly any limit to what man's mind can encompass and produce to enrich and comfort all men on earth.

Nabokov Remembered*

It was not, and still is not, the practice for a teacher to introduce his own accomplishment to a new class, or we would have known, that September day in 1945 when Vladimir Nabokov** walked in, that he was the author of a series of outstanding novels in Russian, that the *New Yorker, Harper's* and *Atlantic Monthly* were publishing his English stories, and critics were celebrating their discovery of a genius. Edmund Wilson, then or soon afterward, called him 'the most extraordinary phenomenon of the kind since Conrad ... something like Proust, something like Franz Kafka, and probably, something like Gogol ... (but) as completely himself as any of these other writers'. Enough and to spare for conceit, and we, with a year or more at Wellesley College in Massachusetts behind us, were quick to detect it where we found it in our teachers. A narcissistic entrant to the philosophy faculty was known among his students as 'God's gift to the Greeks' since he clearly believed that was what he was. If there was any trace of conceit about Mr Nabokov, we never saw it.

---

* *Span,* February 1978

** The recent death of Vladimir Nabokov evokes memories in an Indian writer of the days when, at a college in Massachusetts, Nabokov unveiled the mysteries of the Russian language in beautifully precise English, recreating the setting of Tsarist Russia with remarkable clarity.

All I knew when he walked in was that his appearance – long, lean and balding, his shoulders slightly raised, slightly hunched, the way he wore his clothes, rather loosely – all in some indefinable way said 'European'. He must have been forty-six years old. The American world around me was new, young, untarnished, measurable in decades. Since my arrival in America a year earlier, the beauty and serenity of Wellesley had seemed almost unbelievable against the war news from Europe and Asia and the imprisoned parents, fighting for freedom, I had left at home. The war had just barely ended, but my father had died of his prison term, and freedom for India was still not in sight. There were times when Wellesley's inhabitants and their concerns looked exquisitely unreal to me. Instinctively I reached out for the anchor of older experience, and was consoled by maturity where I found it, more often in my books and teachers than in my fellow students. I thought Mr Nabokov handsome. It would have been a wildly improbable thing to say in a teenage environment where handsomeness was crew-cut, upturned-nosed, suitably muscular, in or just out of uniform, always and invariably young and preferably marriageable. So I didn't say it.

We sat, fifteen or twenty of us – a lot for a language class, and Russian at that, at a long table, and after the preliminaries Mr Nabokov walked to the blackboard – we discovered he almost never sat down – and wrote on it in English script the Russian word 'kneega.' He said the word lingeringly out loud, and asked us to repeat it several times. 'Do you *like* it?' he demanded. 'Is it *pleasing* to you?' It meant, we learned, book. We learned more than its meaning. It taught us to join two consonants, an exercise alien to the Anglo-Saxon tongue, though familiar to me. And unlike words in English, it had no accented syllable, which was the way of most Russian words. Every syllable counted. So, for Mr Nabokov, did the music of words, and he sometimes read us a passage we did not understand for its lilt, for the rhythm and pace of the Russian sentence, and a broad grasp of the way Russian sounded. There were no technical aids or short cuts to the teaching of language then, except linguaphone records which we did not use, and we had to plod along with grammar, declensions, conjugations and the solid business of memorizing vocabulary. If the teacher could not convey the feel of language, learning was a dull business. Our class was too fast-paced and full of variety to be dull. Mr Nabokov, who talked a lot, was very much at home with words. He spoke the beautifully precise and idiomatic English of the cultivated north European, the kind that once distinguished the upper classes in Russia, and now is only spoken outside England by the Swedes. He carried his own English sentences, especially the descriptive ones, to their destination and then around the corner. His use of language had that faculty of opening up a new vista quite suddenly when you thought you had seen what you came to see. I found it later in his writing of the period, in the stories he was sending to literary magazines while he taught us beginning Russian. Take this sentence from *Signs and Symbols:* 'She presented a naked white countenance to the fault-finding light of spring days,' introducing an image and then, unexpectedly, another. This onward-going two-image construction was fascinating to me. The only analogy I have been able to find for it, much later, lies in scenery, not language, and only in Kashmir, where in the width and expanse of the valley, a turn in the road you are travelling can confront you with a vivid new sight.

Mr Nabokov could, in our teenage lingo, be 'hilarious'. 'Take the Russian verb "ostanavlivat".' he said, 'which means "to stop". In the days of the horse carriage it was all right to shout "ostanavlivaite" to a man about to cross the street, to save him from an oncoming vehicle. But in our automobile culture the poor fellow would get run over before the warning was out, so nowadays it is customary to say "stop".' Some words, he told us, become international with use, like 'bifshtek' or 'djaz'.

I had entered the class with an advantage. Loving languages, I had started Russian the previous summer with a gifted eccentric teacher who had a nervous breakdown every few years under the strain of teaching fourteen languages. I could already read simple Russian and converse in it. I did not deserve Mr Nabokov's casual remark to a colleague, conveyed I do not remember how to me, that 'Mees Pandit' was the most brilliant and beautiful girl in his class. But I cherished the compliment and became more expansive in class.

I don't know how aware Wellesley was that it sheltered at the time two giant reputations-in-the-making: in the Spanish department, Jorge Guillen, who was to win the Spanish-speaking world's most prestigious literary prize in 1976, and Vladimir Nabokov, who in a few years, with the publication of *Lolita,* would win international acclaim and be able to devote himself exclusively to writing. My 1947 yearbook makes no mention of either and does not even list a Russian department.

I used to meet Senor Guillen in corridors. Did everyone look tall to me because I was young and small? Or was he actually as tall as I remember him, with a humorous gleam in place of a smile, eyes that closed when he talked, books under one arm, bending his head to talk to a colleague or a student? I knew him only at greeting distance. Spanish was taught to me that year by Senorita Oyarzabal, a frail, angular, aristocratic refugee from Franco's Spain, whose love for her country was overlaid by a bitter nostalgia. I wanted to weep in her class. Such a sadness clung even to Spanish verbs under her guidance. Far from home myself I was acutely conscious of her yearning for her promised land, country of countries, home, Spain, of which all that was left to her now, and perhaps forever, was memory. I understood the Senorita in my bones, and thought of the irony of a world where some dictators were destroyed and others flourished, driving good people from their homes.

I knew Mr Nabokov was a refugee too, of longer standing than my Spanish teacher. Asides and explanations during the stories we studied in class lit up the life he had left: the huge country estate he had lived on as a boy, complete with footmen and maids, governesses and tutors; the trips to Europe, French culture and English learning lying like lace frills on the surrounding Russian fabric. He did not indulge in continuous recall of this kind. It came out where it was relevant to what we might be reading at the time. He never told us his family had left Russia soon after the Revolution, never to return, and that his father had been assassinated in 1922, the year he took his degree in modern languages from Trinity College, Cambridge. And except that he had travelled a lot, lived in England as a student, in Germany and France and then in America, there was nothing of the homeless wanderer about him, nothing of drama or disaster, no smear of self-pity or anger, not a single suggestion that an entire past had been wiped out behind him.

I knew a Russian émigré family who lived near Wellesley. The Berestneffs were warm-hearted, hospitable extroverts. At Russian Easter the Russian wife of an American foreign correspondent I knew took me to a party at their house. Sixteen then, I had never been to such a party. They ate and drank Russian delicacies, wine and vodka, sang Russian songs to the accompaniment of a balalaika with an emotional extravagance that swept me off my feet. Mr Berestneff took my hand and charmed me into dancing with him. Yet as the evening wore on, a haunting melancholy pervaded the festivity. These were people who had never left Russia, and never would. All else was wilderness and exile. It left an indelible impression on me. This was what being driven from one's own soil did to people. They drifted and pined. The outer framework of their lives, though they might spend the rest of their lives in it, remained outer. Shadows became real, and the real never took firm shape. The troop ship I had come to America on – no passenger ships were crossing torpedoed seas then – had carried 700 Polish refugees, immigrants who had the look of dry shed leaves waiting for another wind. Those had been poor, destitute people, while the Berestneffs were privileged and cultured. But their plight seemed oddly similar, oddly futureless. I had not then met Mr Nabokov.

When I did, I could not imagine him at the Berestneffs. I don't know if he knew them. There was an intellectual exactitude about him that did not wallow in anything. He was brisk and energetic. He walked miles in that classroom. He had no mannerism we could get hold of, no obvious way of talking or gesticulating, nothing to label 'foreign' or quaint that would relegate him to a collector's item among teachers. He had a quick sympathetic smile for atrocious pronunciation, charity for our mistakes, and a kindly interest in our efforts. But he did not spill over onto us. Student–teacher rapport of the sort now considered a necessity was not a violent need or demand in those days. There was a generation gap and there was expected to be one. A society, its ages and stages of life all glued together in a heart-to-heart association, would have seemed hideous and preposterous. I don't know if any student had an outside-class, come-to-my-house relationship with Mr Nabokov. I did not and I don't believe any such existed. Even in class his teaching had a trim and tailored elegance. He did not go into transports, and he did not allow words or ideas to go on a spree. Senorita Oyarzabal got carried away with passages of the Spanish poets. She reminisced while she taught. It was part of the wistful spell she wove. With Mr Nabokov we remained with the lesson. Yet, if we were reading an extract from Pushkin's *Queen of Spades* or lines from a Lermontov poem, we 'saw' the scene as he explained it to us in detailed visual miniatures recreating the vanished setting of Tsarist Russia with its high bourgeoisie, and its hard-drinking, duelling officer class. We saw it as in a mirror, or framed in wood, or glimpsed through an archway, alive and peopled, but confined to its own space and time, not intruding on ours. He filled us in with wit and a clear eye on the background, history or personality we were reading about, but it was *there* and we were *here*, and there was no confusing the two. For the first time I dimly understood – though the understanding did not serve me till later when I began to write – that fact and fiction, 'here' and 'there', were different, two realms, and for the fastidious artist must always remain so. It may have been this capacity to be so actively in the present himself that made Mr Nabokov un-refugee-like. An ironic half sentence from his story, 'A Forgotten Poet' – 'no matter whether the Tsar be called Alexander, Nicholas, or Joe' – succinctly reveals his devastating detachment for what it really was, the sense of history that kept him whole and healthy, both as human being and writer. Another half sentence at the end of 'Mademoiselle O' as surely puts all literary detachment in its proper place, at the far end of heartbreak, not something separate and distinct from the aching, feeling process: 'I catch myself wondering whether, during the years I knew her, I had not kept utterly missing something in her . . . something, in short, that I could appreciate only after the things and beings that I had most loved in the security of my childhood had been turned to ashes or shot through the heart.' Perhaps only the indomitable among writers and men can rebuild in fiction a world irrevocably lost with so clean and uncluttered a vision, and only a handful of the creative can invent, as Nabokov did, a whole new world on the ashes of the old.

By the time I began to read Nabokov, he had made America peculiarly, breathtakingly, his own. I was not surprised that this encounter did not reflect the voice of the immigrant, or the more sophisticated émigré, or echoes of any other lifetime. This was life in its own right, conveyed in language that was nothing if not lyrically, startlingly original. Of all those who have loved English and made it their own, Nabokov's use of it has seemed to me the most enriching – the result almost of a meeting between two civilizations, rather than an artist and a new medium, or an exile and a foreign tongue.

As We Once Were*

Extraordinary human quality is a rare discovery in our tin-and-tinsel era of money-madness and mindless consumerism when success is reckoned by market value, idealism is extinct and heroes are hard to come by in India's public life. But I met one in Johannesburg last September. I was there to take part in a cultural festival marking 'The Indian Experience in South Africa' but this meeting was not on the programme. It was my good fortune that a friend arranged for me to meet Albie Sachs. He is seventy-three years old, a judge in the country's highest court, known as Constitutional Court, and one who played a leading role in writing the Constitution that transformed a tyrannical racist state into one of justice and human rights for all. Much is known and repeatedly recalled about the Holocaust, but so little is remembered about the evil decades of apartheid that the man I was waiting to meet in the spacious front room of the court is not as well known in India as he should be. Albie Sachs started life as a privileged white South African, became a civil rights lawyer and an activist member of the African National Congress and thereby a target for assassination as one of the apartheid regime's most wanted 'race traitors'. He was twice imprisoned in the mid-1960s, during one term for 167 days of solitary confinement and torture in a soundproof cell. In

---

* *Outlook*, 2008

1988 in exile in Mozambique, he was nearly killed when he was car-bombed by agents of the South African security forces. His right arm was blown off and he lost the sight of one eye. He went through surgeries for widespread internal damage and then spent many months in hospital, learning to make his mutilated body function without help and his mind to cope with the horror of his situation. Mere survival would have been hard enough to achieve in these grim circumstances. The last thing I expected to see was the tall upright man striding vigorously towards me and the last thing I expected to find in him was a calm and optimistic view of life and his country's future. His recovery has in fact, been so awe-inspiring that a few years ago he fell in love, remarried, and now has a child.

Talking to him in his office it was clear that non-violence as a working creed is well and alive in men such as him, his great comrade Mandela, and countless others who had repaid atrocious persecution with the offer of reconciliation. When the Truth and Reconciliation Commission held its hearings, at which thousands of apartheid victims told their stories, and a smaller number of evildoers seeking amnesty in return for truth told theirs, Albie Sachs had not taken his case to the Commission. He saw the TRC primarily as serving a socio-moral purpose and much needed emotional release for those who could break their silence at long last, and not as providing reparation for the incalculable harm done – for how could any reparation be measured against what people had suffered? His way of dealing with his own case was to bring an end to the country's tortured past through its new Constitution which would make way for the democratic society his assassins would not allow, and thereby 'to show the superiority of our values over theirs'. 'No feelings of vengeance?' he had been asked. Surprisingly, none. He replied that the bomb or something like it was bound to happen. He had made his choices and known the risks he was taking. 'Ever since I was seventeen and sat down on a seat marked Blacks Only, I have been preparing myself for some confrontation with apartheid power.' His own 'vengeance' had taken the form of helping to create the framework for a rule of law – particularly necessary in his opinion for the poor and powerless – that would bring blacks and whites together for the first time as equal citizens with a shared future history. President Mandela recalled the divided history of the past when he inaugurated the Constitutional Court, saying, 'The last time I stood up in court was to find out if I was going to be hanged.'

If ever architecture fulfilled its purpose as the centrepiece of a new government's high ideals, it is Constitutional Court. Far from imposing, it looks informal, welcoming and full of light. In contrast with conventional court arrangements it reverses the protocol of judges handing down justice from a raised platform while the people in court sit at a lower level. Here the judges sit below – in the service of justice, as it were – and the people higher up. Through a glass panel in an outer wall one can see the black and white legs of passers-by, as a reminder of the people whom justice is there to serve. One corridor in the building is an art gallery displaying the works of South African artists, an aspect of beauty no other court has thought of including.

Part of the building is constructed with bricks taken from the notorious prisons of the apartheid era which are in the same premises. This site has been deliberately chosen as a constant reminder that no human being must ever again be subjected to inhuman treatment. All these jails are maintained as they were, with the addition of pictures and news items from the period, videotapes and guides, as memorials to what South Africans went through. The day I was there, busloads of schoolchildren were being shown around them. One of these jails has the distinction of being the only one in the world that has held both Gandhi and Mandela. The whole precincts, now known as Constitution Hill, will have the biggest human rights library in the country and provide amenities for scholars and human rights activists. The same meticulous care for preserving the past accurately has been taken in setting up the Apartheid Museum in Johannesburg and in retaining the original look and ambience of the railway station in Pietermaritzburg where the young Gandhi was thrown out of a train for occupying a 'whites only' compartment.

I found my visit a profoundly moving experience for all that it conveyed of a country using the bricks and memories of its tormented past imaginatively to create a new tradition of equality and justice. India, in contrast, has shown neither interest nor talent for preserving its recent past. No prison that held our freedom fighters has even a plaque to commemorate a historic era. The jail here in Dehra Dun where Jawaharlal Nehru occupied one of three cells in 1932-33, and where my father, Ranjit Pandit, shared imprisonment with him in 1940-41, has now been demolished to make way for 'development' – though I am told that those three cells, which were outside the main jail, have been left standing. I hope this will not also be torn down in due course in the rush for 'development'. In a travesty of truth, Veer Savarkar's portrait now hangs in Parliament House in an alcove opposite the Mahatma's, ranking with the men and women who laid the foundations of modern India. With this kind of destruction and falsification of the best of our past and all that it stood for, what can we expect of the present but exactly what is happening – the distortion of religious and regional identity, an epidemic of fanaticism leading to the slaughter of Christians in Orissa, the lynching of young Bihari workers in Mumbai, and a vicious intolerance for the views of others in life and in art. The gap between vast wealth and dire poverty that makes two nations of us and the soar to superpower status without a garbage disposal system on the ground are two more aspects of forgetting what we once regarded as priorities. And there is no one now to remind us of what they were. With understandable pride we are headed for the moon, but few among us are still reaching for the stars

PART FIVE

To, By and About Me

Two Letters from Gopalkrishna Gandhi

Raj Bhavan, Kolkata
30 March 2007

Dear Nayantara

Today's dak has brought the lovely gift of your novel. May I deserve it – and its deeply moving inscription. Thank you.

I cannot say adequately through the vehicle of words what your phone call meant. And I want you to know I have followed your advice – felt and I hope looked more confident than before.

Keep well.
As always and sincerely with love,
Gopal

Raj Bhavan, Kolkata
20 June 2007

Dear Nayantara

To know that you were staying at the IIC when Ramu died places a poultice over my ache.

Thank you for writing. It means more than I can say in words.

I am so glad he was there at the launch of *Before Freedom*. I can imagine him enjoying the event.

Love as alwys,
Gopal

Letter from Shyam Benegal

Shyam Benegal

PRODUCTION OFFICE:
19/-20A, EVEREST
TARDEO ROAD
BOMBAY 400 034.
Phones: 494 3977, 494 2435

January 10, 1990.

Ms. Nayantara Sahgal,
181-B Rajpur Road,
DEHRADUN - 248009.

Dear Ms. Sahgal,

I read your novel 'Mistaken Identity' with great interest. It is an excellent piece of work. I loved the period character and the cleverly designed structure of the story. More than that, you have succeeded in placing your finger on the pulse of that time - the varying attitudes and motivations of people; the class, caste and communal biases. It will certainly make an engaging film.

Now for the practical part: Ideally, the film should be bilingual; characters speaking in English or Hindi as the occasion demands it. I am not sure how well this would be received, but it is worth a try. There are two ways to present it; either as a mini-series for Television or as a Cinema film. Funding for film is not too easy these days so I would rather attempt it as a mini-series in three or four episodic parts of one hour each.

If you are willing, I can send a proposal to Doordarshan along these lines. Before that, however, I would like to know the manner in which you would like to participate in the project. What kind of royalty would you expect and whether you would be willing to write or collaborate on the script.
Do let me know.

Kind regards,

Yours sincerely,

(SHYAM BENEGAL)

Note: This proposal never came about.

Letter from Mani Shankar Aiyar

Mani Shankar Aiyar
Minister, Panchayati Raj, Youth Affairs & Sports, and
Development of the North Eastern Region
Government of India, New Delhi
8 March 2007

Dear dear Nayantara,

Thanks a million for your lovely letter of 5 March and the cover of *A Time To Be Happy*. I have crossed page 200, and am quite as excited as when I read the book the better part of half a century ago. It is a quite remarkably evocative portrait of a page from our history that has virtually disappeared from our collective memory. I caught the fag end of that era and then, as now, I am moved almost to tears by the way a vanished world is brought back to life by your felicitous pen. Congratulations!

Your secular scoundrel,
Mani

Note: Mani' s sign-off refers to my letter to the editor of *Gahrwal Post*, Dehra Dun, dated 5 March 2007, in which I say:

'... If, for the sake of argument, all politicians are scoundrels, I would always choose the secular scoundrel, since what I hold most dear in India – our multi-faceted identity – is safer in secular hands.'

Letter from Anita Desai

10 Parsonage Street, Cold Spring, NY 10516
25 October 2006

Dear Nayantara,

It was so very kind of you to think of sending me the clippings from the Indian newspapers which I of course don't see here, and which gave me so much joy. I feel I was so extraordinarily lucky to be in Dehra Dun just when the news of the Booker Prize broke; nowhere else could the joy have been more personally felt than in India. All those captions 'An Honour for India' and 'Kiran Does India Proud' made it seem the country was rejoicing along with me. It was as if the cricket team had won a series!

The other wonderful thing was how simply everyone I have ever known in my life and travels managed to get in touch and convey their congratulations. It was like a reaching out of hands across the world. I was so touched and only wished Kiran could have been with me to experience it instead of in London or Frankfurt or New York, being worried to death by the media and just wanting to crawl into bed and sleep.

Your telephone call was a part of all that joy and celebration. I'm sorry I had to cut it short on account of all the phones in the house – and everyone seems to have three or four of them – ringing at the same time.

The next time I am in Dehra Dun I shall certainly take up your invitation and come to see you. This had been only a very brief trip of three days and those three days were swamped by the news and its aftermath. I am sure the next visit will be quieter.

I would have loved to hear more about you and the books you have been writing and publishing; do feel very cut off from the Indian scene living here in the US where one feels more and more isolated and cut off from the rest of the world as it is. I had been in Bali for a book festival and envied the to and fro between all the countries of SE Asia evident there, and that exists in Europe of course and also, separately, in Latin America. It is so entirely missing in the US – and perhaps in India too?

So we should take every opportunity to get in touch and stay in touch. I intend to.

Yours, with love,
Anita

Letter from A. Ranganathan

A. Ranganathan
Locksley Hall East
852 Poonamallee High Road, Kilpauk, Madras - 600010
12 October 1979

My dear Nayantara,

I was deeply moved by your piece 'A Memorial for JP' (*Indian Express,* 11 October 1979). You are right in stating that JP 'was in a class by himself ... He was transparently true and whole.' Think JP was a great fighting idealist. By the way, he made a reference to you in one of his speeches in Madras (it was sometime in 1976): Characteristically, this reference to you was meaningful and yet impersonal. He was happy that a writer like you was getting involved in politics: 'It augurs well for the country that a writer like Nayantara Sahgal is currently involving herself in the politics of dissent.'

I do hope that you will contest a seat for the Lok Sabha during the forthcoming election.

You have my good wishes.
With all good wishes and kindest regards,

Yours sincerely,
Rangu

Letter from Jagat Mehta

CONFIDENTIAL/ PERSONAL

विदेश सचिव
विदेश मंत्रालय, नई दिल्ली-११
FOREIGN SECRETARY
MINISTRY OF EXTERNAL AFFAIR
NEW DELHI-11

No. F. 49/2183/NGO

June 25, 1979

My dear Tara

The President, Prime Minister and the Foreign Minister have approved of your nomination as our Ambassador to Italy. I need hardly say that this reflects the confidence in your ability, diplomatic sagacity and standing in Public life. Our political relations with Italy have always been free of friction. Our economic relations with this important member of the European Economic Community have recently been developing well but sustained effort will be necessary to realise its fuller potential.

2. Rome, as you know, is the headquarters of one of the most important UN agencies viz. Food and Agriculture Organisation. Our Ambassador is expected to maintain close cooperation with the higher echelons of this Organisation which is important from the point of view of our national programmes and priorities.

3. Many formalities have to be completed including obtaining the Agre-ment of the receiving government. Other details like timings of the move etc. could be discussed later. I might add that Mr. Damodaran, who is at present our Ambassador in Rome, has been given an extension upto the end of December, 1979.

4. I hope it may be possible for you to take up the appointment. Meanwhile, the decision must be kept strictly confidential until it is announced.

With kind regards,

Yours sincerely

(J.S.Mehta)

Smt. Nayantara Sehgal,
10, Massey Hall,
Jai Singh Road,
NEW DELHI-110001.

Note: My appointment by the Janata government as ambassador to Italy was cancelled by Indira Gandhi when she returned to power in 1980.

Letter from Jayaprakash Narayan

जयप्रकाश नारायण
JAYAPRAKASH NARAYAN

दूरभाष : ५१२३९
Telephone : 5 1 2 3 9

कदमकुआँ * पटना–८००००३ * बिहार * भारत
Kadamkuan * Patna-800003 * Bihar * India

Dated 30.5.1978

Dear Tara,

I have heard several chapters of your new book, Indira Gandhi's Emergence and Style, which you were kind enough to send to me. I treat it as a significant contribution to contemporary political literature on national affairs and admire your dispassionate approach to a rather personally delicate theme. I have no doubt the book will prove very helpful in understanding and appreciating the developments in the last ten to fifteen years in the country.

With love and best wishes,

Yours affly,
Jayaprakash
(Jaya Prakash Narayan)

To

Mrs. Nayan Tara Sahgal,
<u>New Delhi</u>

Two Letters from John Kenneth Galbraith

JOHN KENNETH GALBRAITH
HARVARD UNIVERSITY
CAMBRIDGE, MASSACHUSETTS

June 13, 1977

Personal

Mme. Vijaya Lakshmi Pandit
181-B Rajpur Road
Dehra Dun, U. P.
India

Dear Nan:

I deeply hope that you will continue the great family tradition and play a role in the years ahead. I was distressed to hear from various underground sources that you are reluctant to come to Washington; nothing would be so good at this juncture as to have a member of your family of indubitably democratic and liberal instinct here in the United States. But perhaps there are more important tasks for you in New Delhi. And this brings me to my subject. Why couldn't Tara be suggested as an ambassador? She is a distinguished novelist, and it is always good to have someone who has made it on her own intellectual and artistic skills. She combines a superb knowledge of Indian politics with a comprehensive knowledge of the United States. She makes friends easily and has many. She is the right age for dealing with the people of the Carter Administration and would command their immediate respect. I make this proposal only as a friend and only to indicate, should there be any doubt, how much it would be welcomed here.

Yours faithfully,

Ken

John Kenneth Galbraith

JKG/laf

Make me a good excuse to come back to India some not distant day. I need [illegible] the excuse!

JOHN KENNETH GALBRAITH
HARVARD UNIVERSITY
CAMBRIDGE

June 11, 1982

Ms. Nayantara Sahgal
10 Massey Hall
Jai Singh Road
New Delhi 110 001
India

Dear Tara:

So many thanks for the book* and yet more for the dedication. I am truly pleased and honored.

So far I've just skimmed but I am settling down to serious reading this very week.

Thanks and love again.

Love,

* *Indira Gandhi: Her Road to Power*

Letter from Howard Gotlieb

BOSTON UNIVERSITY

CHENERY LIBRARY
725 Commonwealth Avenue, BOSTON, MASSACHUSETTS 02215

August 10, 1966

Mrs. Nayantara Sahgal
E-8, Mafattal Park
Bhulabai Desai Road
Bombay 26, India

Dear Mrs. Sahgal:

I am sure that many institutions have been in contact with you asking that they might become the repository of your manuscripts and correspondence files. I write to say that Boston University would be honored to establish a Nayantara Sahgal Collection, and to plead our particular cause for these reasons.

We are in the midst of building a magnificent new library on our Charles River Campus and we hope to make this library a center of study and research in contemporary literature. Up to the present time Boston University has been growing so rapidly as a "national" institution, that we have waited until we were ready with the proper facilities before establishing such a literary research center. With the advent of our new building we are now ready to embark upon this project.

It is our hope to collect the papers of outstanding contemporary literary figures, house and curate these materials under the optimum archival conditions, and attract to us scholars in the field of contemporary literature who would utilize our institution as a research base.

Your papers would be preserved for future generations. I do hope that you will look sympathetically upon our request. May I say personally how much I have enjoyed your published work.

Sincerely yours,

Howard B. Gotlieb

Howard B. Gotlieb
Chief of Reference and
Special Collections.
Boston University Libraries

HBG:mr

Note: My papers, until the 1980s, were purchased for Howard Gotlieb's Special Archives. The rest have been gifted to the Nehru Memorial Museum and Library at Teen Murti Bhavan, New Delhi.

PART SIX

Miscellany

Randolph with Love*

I met Randolph in London before the world changed beyond recognition. It was the summer of 1955. Except that the British Empire had called it a day and decolonization had been set in motion, the world was pretty much as it had been for as long as anyone could remember, with its established etiquettes and its unwritten rules. In spite of the war's upheavals Fred Astaire could still have sung as he did in *Top Hat* in the 1930s during my parents' youth:

I'm stepping out, my deah
Into an atmospheah
That simply reeks of class...

Caste and class were securely in place. So were the sexes, each in his or hers. Men wore hats and raised them to women, drew out chairs for them and made way for them to pass, in return for ruling the roost. Dancing was done in pairs, romantically close or amiably inches apart. In a manner of speaking social life resembled the Englishman in the jungle who dressed for dinner nevertheless. Blushing was not unknown. Private life stayed private. The main rule, I think, was that one did not transgress boundaries. The young Queen's younger sister broke her own heart rather than tradition

* This piece was written in memory of my good friend, Randolph Boxall, who died a few years ago, for his wife, Marjorie Boxall.

when she gave up Group Captain Townsend in deference to what the Church and the public expected of royal behaviour.

It was a time when actors and actresses kept their clothes on, yet passion managed to get powerfully conveyed on stage and screen. There were breasts, bottoms and pelvises as ever, but they stayed parts of bodies and did not launch out on their own to win laurels as freelancers. Entertainment was entertaining. I saw *CanCan* and *Kismet* that season, and *That Reluctant Debutante.* Debutantes still came 'out' and were presented at court. Adultery was very delicately broached in '*The Grass in Greener*'.

There were no electronic devices to make noise out of music and to carry performing voices to a punishing pitch. I remember an evening at the Café de Paris in London where Marlene Dietrich was performing solo. She was then fifty-four years old, clothed from neck to ankles, not an inch of flesh showing, and she stood motionless. Even her lips hardly moved as she half huskily sang, half spoke the songs she had made famous in a voice that a reviewer later described as champagne poured along a gravel path. Her performance was generally acclaimed for its unrivalled glamour and sexual allure and I haven't seen one to match it since.

It all come back to me, living proof of how era-spanning friendship can be, this one starting in that lull before liberty, equality and fraternity burst upon Britain with a bang and transformed society, politics and sex. I was in England for the first time, on a visit to my mother who was India's high commissioner to the Court of St. James. It was still the country I had learned about through nursery rhymes, processions of kings and their wars and the like that Britain's occupation of my country had made compulsory in schools. Rebels against the Empire like my parents had spent years of their lives in prison for working to overthrow that occupation. This done, we could fall in love with England with a clear conscience and I proceeded to do so. A friend took me to Randolph's bachelor flat where we had a drink before going out to dinner, I forget where, and on other evenings to nightclubs called Annabel's and Churchill's – all high spots I took in my stride not having the faintest idea how select they were. It was always somewhere grand because I went in saris of Benares silk and gold and silver tissue, and jewellery to match. I also had a coat from Harvey Nichols, tiny-waisted with a flared skirt, that seemed designed to wear over a sari. And Randolph came often to the Indian embassy at my mother's invitation.

I had no idea then how durable this acquaintance was going to prove since I could only renew it on rare visits to London. Once in 1959 Randolph and a friend of his took me and my sister Rita pub-crawling. In 1972 when I was taking my daughter Gita to Atlantic College in Wales, he took us to lunch at his club. But when my visits became frequent in the 1980s, and 47 Gloucester Ave opened its hospitable doors and became home to me, I entered on a second- and then, with the arrival of Kabir and Zum, a third-generation relationship with the Boxalls. I had the guest room upstairs and was a much indulged guest. They lived in the garden flat below, each of them fully engaged with work of their own – Marjorie with her sculpture and writing, Randolph with the enormous task of renovating their mansion – yet both of them inexhaustibly involved with their near- and far-flung friends.

I suppose what I remember as most typical of Randolph is that unlike many of us as we grow older he didn't order his life differently, didn't in any way diminish. He stayed himself exactly, only older, enjoying his pleasures: Food! Cooking it, he and Marjorie, in all its variety, including making successful puris and the best prawn curry outside Goa. Drink! All sorts from Europe's wines to the Indian champagne with which we toasted Kabir's birth. Foregathering with friends, young, old and very young, when affection was so visibly demonstrated in so many ways, extending to one's children and grandchildren and the friends of friends. Laughter at the dining table, whether the subject was his half-truck with feminism, his no-truck with socialism, or hilarity over what royalty had come to with its topless antics. Britain was by then barely recognizable as the country I had met him in. But some things remained the same. 'I'm going to City Livery Company dinner tonight,' he wrote to me on 12 January 2000, 'I haven't worn white tie for many years and have become much fatter since the trousers were made for me. I was wearing this outfit when I first met Marjorie and they prove she has got more than she bargained for!' And his letters always began 'Our very dear Tara'.

The dividing line between Randolph's country and mine had disappeared into history early on in our acquaintance without our ever noticing it. We had adopted each other's and in time become connected in all the ways that count. In any case one's true country is wherever one's friends are. You might say 47 Gloucester Ave became mine.

Chandigarh*

India is so old that we sometimes forget how young its youngest city is, and why there is a city by the name of Chandigarh at all.

Years before any such place had even been thought of, India had been torn apart through the shock called Partition. We know the facts – that Bengal and Punjab were divided to make a new nation, Pakistan – but it is hard, so long after the event, to recall the suffering that both Indians and Pakistanis went through at the time when millions of them were uprooted from their homes, with nowhere to go and nothing to look forward to. Many of them must have been haunted by the terrifying sights they had seen and the dangers they had faced during the Partition riots.

The slice of Punjab that had been left with India needed a capital because the old capital, Lahore, was now in Pakistan. A new one would need to be built. And it would have to be built from scratch. A city would have to come up out of nothing, in the same way that a story is constructed, or a poem, when you take a blank sheet of paper, let your imagination go to work, and start putting words upon the page. Constructing anything starts in the mind, whether it is a bridge you are building, or a skyscraper or a sonnet. It starts

* Commissioned by Penguin Books, India for a book *Talk of the Town: Stories of Twelve Indian Cities* co-authored by Jerry Pinto and Rahul Srivastava, published in Puffin, September 2008

like an itch in your mind – some would call it inspiration – and makes you get down to the hard labour of bringing that itch of an idea to life.

Chandigarh too started as an idea and those who were imagining it knew it was going to be different from any city in India, first of all because it would be brand new, and this alone would set it apart from the rest of India's towns and cities, most of them full of historic landmarks, from ancient monuments to ancient trees, and other reminders of their long histories. But what would make it truly different would be the new beginning this city would symbolize for a province whose people had lost their homes and livelihoods and hopes and dreams of the future. Bricks and mortar can't make up for the loss of a whole past – all the sights, sounds, surroundings and memories that add up to what we think of as 'home' – but the solid business of construction, of laying brick upon brick, can hold out the promise that life does go on after death and destruction, and that there is always a future for people who are brave enough to build one. That was the kind of promise Chandigarh was meant to be.

A world-famous French architect, Le Corbusier, was chosen to convert this dream into reality. He was invited to India where he drew up plans for the city-to-be and designs for its important public buildings. He had a team of Indian and European architects working under him and it soon became clear that Chandigarh was going to have a look and feel and personality all its own. When I first saw it in 1960 it had been mathematically laid out with broad avenues and city centres. It had a rose garden, a rock garden and a lake, and nature had gifted it with a range of lovely low hills. Le Corbusier's high court building reminded me of pictures I had seen of massive antique Egyptian temples. His legislative assembly building where Punjab's elected politicians would meet to make laws didn't look like any state parliament I had ever seen. This was startling architecture and it made for a lot of discussion and debate. Some people liked it, some didn't, but everybody argued about it. It made people take a fresh look at the city coming up around them and it shook them loose from old set-and-fixed ideas about how buildings should look and how they should be furnished. When private homes came to be built, some owners became adventurous enough to use bold bright colours for interior and outer decoration, which had only been used in village homes before. Whether they realized it or not, citizens were being stimulated by the architecture around them, which is exactly what art and music and architecture, or a novel, should do for people: give them a new way of looking at things. In time the people who settled in Chandigarh began to think of themselves as rather special, and not only because of its originality. In the process of living there they had become what most Indians are not – civic-minded. They cared enough about their city to observe its laws and keep it clean. It is true that other cities have long, proud histories, but Chandigarh must be the only city in India whose citizens are proud enough of it to keep it clean!

Chandigarh became a personal experience for me when my husband built a house in Sector 5 on the boulevard facing the lake, designed by Le Corbusier's cousin and one of his team. Pierre Jeanneret was a genius and geniuses have some strange ideas.The house he built had a huge ramp instead of a staircase. I wanted a staircase. We quarrelled, he in half French, half English. 'Le ramp est magnifique. Le ramp is the signature of the house. It stays.' I'm glad I lost the argument and the ramp stayed. It gives the house its unique 'Chandigarh' look, and is probably the reason why my uncle Jawaharlal Nehru named it Anokha.

Discovering Bimal Roy*

The 1950s are no ordinary decade of time past. They were the years that laid the foundations of the republic. Universal suffrage was put to the test in two general elections. Parliamentary democracy took root, and all the democratic institutions and practices we now take so much for granted were established during the decade. There was something in the air and it was more than the excitement of being in charge of one's own destiny at last and in a position to make things happen. It was the rare brand of optimism that goes with new beginnings. It made for a sense of adventure, and a state of mind and feeling that saw no divide between ideals and their practical application. There was a desire to put right ancient wrongs, and to restore dignity and opportunity to those who had been left out of human consideration and calculation for centuries and this was backed by programmes and policies. Looking back, that period of our recent history does seem framed in a special light. Maybe I thought so because I was young, with a passionate belief in the miracles that Indians, now free, could accomplish. The arts captured the Left- wing mood, and the cinema it created made its impact on audiences with stories, songs and settings that did without myth and fantasy, glamour, gloss and frills. In a departure

---

* Commissioned for publication by Bimal Roy's daughter. Published in *Bimal Roy: The Man Who Spoke in Pictures*, Penguin Books India, 2011.

from the styles and techniques of popular entertainment, it found different dramatic uses for the camera and focused on a different breed of hero: the men and the women who in one way or another were up against the tyrannies of convention and tradition or the furies of the powers that be. Or so I heard from those who were conversant with the new tide.

Being fairly ignorant of what was happening in cinema myself, and only an occasional watcher, I did not see *Do Bigha Zameen* when it came out, though I heard that it went on to win critical acclaim abroad and in time to achieve the status of a classic. I don't know what I expected when I first saw it at home on DVD in 2008 but its deep and devastating pessimism came to me as a shock. It is the story of a peasant who loses his small landholding to his zamindar and whose desperate efforts to retain it bring him and his family to utter ruin. The tale of peasant suffering and sacrifice is not new. It has been told before, and its black-and-white portrayal of good and evil, virtue against vice, is familiar. The characters are hardy perennials: the cruel zamindar, the heartless moneylender, the hapless indebted peasant – but in *Do Bigha Zameen* it becomes a saga of unrelieved misery and defeat. There is not a glimmer of light or hope in the telling. You know that things are never going to get better. I wondered how such an uncompromising pessimism, with not even a glimmer of better times to come, could have come out of the 1950s, when the national mood was generally hopeful and upbeat. The film's pervasive darkness at first seems out of step with the spirit of its time, which both in art and life saw rebellion as the way to fight injustice. However formidable a fate, it could be changed by a refusal to accept it. But rebellion doesn't work for Shambhu, the villager, and fate keeps the upper hand, as it often does in real life.

Real life is, of course, the material of art, and its literal transference to film as 'social realism' was part of an artistic climate fuelled by political and social consciousness. In literature too fiction told it like it was, through straightforward narrative and fidelity to fact, for the ideology of realism did not allow for flights of fancy. In *Do Bigha Zameen* Bimal Roy seems to have given it its harshest interpretation. In a cinema that had until then been hidebound by traditional themes and treatments, starkness comes to the screen through the images his camera chooses to dwell on. The songs, in one of which the villagers sing 'We make everything but nothing is ours', make his political philosophy clear. I had been looking for nuance, for some shading of character in the film, some sequence that would break the monotone effect, until I realized I had been looking for the wrong things, for what I was intended to see was tragedy personified: people who in the nature of things could not alter their circumstances no matter how hard they tried. Shambhu, the beleaguered peasant, tries. He goes to the city for work and becomes a rickshaw puller. He leaves no stone unturned in his back-breaking efforts to lift himself out of debt, save his two bighas and secure his future. Events follow each other in quick succession but every effort he makes meets a dead end, because doom is written into the script. Given the situation he and his kind have been born into, he cannot win. I, the viewer, am being asked to understand that Shambhu cannot change his fate. Only my awareness of his predicament and my roused conscience can make a difference to his life. Ultimately, only a sensitive society and its laws can empower him. Individual effort, however heroic, cannot prevail against an entrenched unequal order.

I recalled that there had, in fact, been a great awareness at government level during the 1950s of the need for grass-roots reform, and far-reaching measures were taken through legislation, for example the Hindu Code Bill, to bring about a much needed social transformation. Another film- maker of the time might have ended the story differently, with perhaps some kind of breathing spell for Shambhu. But every artist's vision comes out of his own private view of the world. Bimal Roy's did not allow for a happy ending or for any respite that would dilute the grimness that he saw as the daily lot of the Indian villager, or indeed for any lightness that would blunt the film's brutal impact on the viewer.

An interesting aspect of the film was the parallels it provides with today. Fifty years on there is still agricultural indebtedness and despair leading to farmers' suicides. The homeless, more and more of them, still sleep on city pavements. Villagers protest rousingly when their land is taken for mills and factories. The moneylender is still a stranglehold power in parts of the coutryside. The trek from rural to urban areas continues, for jobs, for reprieve, for salvation. The present might well be a surreal extension of Bimal Roy's sombre view that nothing was going to get better. Are we then living in the mixture as before? Not at all – we have come a long way since the 1950s – but I found the film with its almost unbearable bleakness disturbing also for its flashes of similarity to today's India and it left me feeling uncomfortable about all that we have failed to deliver.

A few weeks after *Do Bigha Zameen* I watched a DVD of *Devdas,* also for the first time, and this too had its surprises. I had not read the famous 1930s novel it was based on, nor had I seen any of the other versions of the film. The leisurely pace at which the story unravels I put down to the fact that, in pursuit of realism, Bimal Roy chose to be true to the pace of the novel itself, opening with a lengthy childhood sequence and going on to sequences as long-drawn-out and detailed in the telling. Not many novels nowadays survive in their entirety on the screen and this film may have been designed to match the slow static pace of feudal life described in the book, as it was then being lived by the zamindar class. The literal transference of book to screen may also have had something to do with its having been made for an era when audiences had a longer attention span for straight storytelling unadorned by song and dance. It is in every sense a period piece, accurately reflecting a novel that gives the impression (in its screen version) of being immovably fixed in its own time/space and even more rigidly in a setting when every aspect of daily life was locked into the strict limits laid down by class, caste and sub-caste, and divided by an iron curtain between the sexes. The austerity of such a social scene and setting – still valid in too many communities – can be redeemed by art if human nature is allowed to take its course on film, as it has done time and again in life, in reckless defiance of the limits laid upon it and regardless of the consequences. The novelist, Sarat Chandra Chatterji, evidently did not stretch his imagination to any such dangerous possibility, so it seems the film must remain bound to the way human behaviour is depicted in the novel. There is a pivotal scene in which Paro risks her reputation by daring to visit Devdas in the night to tell him she loves him so that he can ask his parents to arrange their marriage. He makes no move towards her, not so much as to touch her hand, or even to look as if he desires her. Concerned that the servants might have seen her, he takes her home. This unconvincing episode puzzles me, where the natural course of human behaviour between childhood friends and would-be lovers has been rejected for an impossibly unreal idea of decorum and gentlemanly conduct. I am not able to believe in this lifeless, sexless Devdas until I get some understanding from a Bengali friend of the romantic tradition that ruled Bengali literature of that period, making a cult of melancholy, of the consumptive, the alcoholic, and whatever spelled loss, defeat and despair. In such a scenario love would have to remain unconsummated, and the quintessential romantic hero would be expected to go into a decline, become an alcoholic, and finally die of drink and a broken heart. If this is the rationale of the story, it gives Bimal Roy ample scope to cast a brooding darkness over its film version, this time the tragedy of lovers trapped in societal conditions that can neither be bent nor escaped. Love cannot conquer all. It cannot be allowed to because, if it did, it would breach the hallowed limits laid down for conduct and destroy the social fabric.

Another Bengali friend pointed out that Sarat Chandra Chatterji was a champion of women. This then accounts for the two impressive women in the story, both of whom have more courage and character than the weak-willed Devdas and know what they want from life and love. But they too are left with no choice but to submit to the roles that society expects of them. Paro, who, driven by passion, goes to Devdas in the night, later resigns herself to an arranged marriage to a much older widower and fulfils her uncomplaining role of dutiful wife and mother to his children. Love for Devdas inspires the courtesan to give up and become the model of a virtuous woman, meekly serving him as a caring companion, if not a wife, and expecting nothing more. She herself believes her 'sinful' past entitles her to nothing more. For neither woman is there a breakthrough into personal happiness or fulfilment. Both must remain bound by the merciless rules that govern the lives of their sex. The helplessness of individuals to overturn embedded tradition is a theme that *Devdas* – like *Do Bigha Zameen* – echoes in another context. Both cry out for society to do more.

The only two Roy films I have now seen have left me curious about Bimal Roy the man and whether the darkness of his vision was confined to his creative output or had something to do with the circumstances of his own life. Like other men and women who left an enduring imprint on their professions in the decade before and just after Independence, he must have been touched by the significance of the transforming times he lived in – but in these two films at least he remained untouched by their optimism. What comes through in black and white, devoid of spectacle and special effects, is mid-twentieth-century India, driven by its aura of idealism and the emotional intensity that converted it into political action and carried it into forms of art.

Friends, This Is India – Hold On!*

The family belonged to the bourgeoisie spawned by British rule. Wealth and stability don't make for a life at the barricades, so drama must have been their fate. It started with my grandfather, Motilal Nehru, whose early success at the Allahabad Bar enabled him in 1900 to buy a mansion in spacious grounds, engage an English-Irish tutor recommended by Annie Besant to prepare his son, Jawaharlal, for Harrow, and later an English governess for his daughters. He didn't send his laundry to Paris as rumoured, but he did invite all the children at his hotel in Baden-Baden to his daughter's fifth birthday party. His hospitality was famous and the patriarchal pride and bounty he lavished on his extended family were princely even by the standards of this hallowed Indian institution.

He loved a fight, from a wrestling bout to intellectual combat, and was mildly contemptuous of the elite assembly known as the Indian National Congress that met once a year at sessions festooned with oratory to petition the sovereign power for greater Indian participation in India's civil and military services, and elbow room for Indian capital in an economy run for British profit. Mainstream politics went no further and Motilal Nehru found it a tame substitute for action.

* *Guardian,* 5 March 1992

A fierier patriotism had sent a string of Indian revolutionaries to the gallows, life imprisonment, death in prison, or agitation abroad. National consciousness smarted under an imperial language of insult and exclusion – 'the subject races' of officialese, the Gunga Din image and white superiority – so secure it did not need the prop of apartheid, but railway carriages, station retiring rooms, clubs and park benches reserved For Europeans Only testified to Herrenvolk and master race.

The lawyers, professors and entrepreneurs of the Congress, however, depended on their dignified petitions to bring out the best in the British. They profoundly believed this buried 'best' would arise and respond, granting India, like the white dominions, self-government and equal status in the Empire. Trustfully they rallied to the Empire's support in Europe's Great War and Gandhi, called Mahatma for the non-violent campaigns he had led in South Africa, himself recruited men for it.

It was after the war, when arbitrary arrest and jail without trial to ensure business as usual were followed on 13 April 1919, by the slaughter at Jallianwala Bagh, a walled garden in Amritsar where General Dyer's troops opened fire without warning on a crowd of thousands celebrating the spring festival, that the national agenda abruptly changed and Gandhi outlined his non-violent strategy for independence. Those who found civil disobedience too daunting or bizarre moved away from the action. Others, including the family, plunged into it.

Here it was that national and family history met, not quite as they must have in many families whose father, son or second cousin joined the fray, loyally supported by those who stayed outside it. In mine, the household, jointly in thrall to a country whose destiny it took to be its own, jointly ended its old life and started its new one. A decade later the connection was rooted, permanent, mysterious. It gave their 'we' and 'ours' a curious breadth and span, considering they couldn't possibly have known they and theirs would in time rule India for close to forty years.

The ABC of their total transformation was traceable. Point four of Gandhi's strategy called on lawyers to give up their practice. Father, son and son-in-law complied. Point nine required men and women 'to make as much sacrifice as possible'. They made a blazing bonfire of their British goods, donated the mansion to the party and moved into a small (by Motilal's patriarchal standards) domed house they built on the same estate. Both houses flew the Congress flag: saffron (for Hinduism) and green (for Islam), divided by a spinning wheel (for cottage industry) on a white (for unity) middle band. Point ten about avoiding abuse as well as violence must have been more of a hurdle since the patriarch had a roaring temper when roused.

He had not reached the heights of his profession by suffering fools gladly or doing as he was told. But those must have been days when lions lay down with lambs, lords and vassals joined forces, worms turned. From infancy on I understood that the family with like-minded others all over the country had fallen into the radical regime of setting up committees in towns and villages, organizing these for political action, wearing and spinning the handspun cloth known as khadi, controlling their tempers, breaking laws and going to jail.

But if so many others were doing all this, then why had 'destiny' struck only us? To be sure it had. I knew I was living in an Age, but which Age was another matter, with all time ever present around us. It was clear enough to our gardener for whom the family's move from the mansion to the domed house was the Ramayana all over again, just like Ram and Sita's halt the other day at the Bharadwaja ashram across the road on their journey into exile after renouncing the throne of Ayodhya.

Renouncing a property and a livelihood, not knowing what tomorrow would bring, had a high-altitude effect on their personalities. My uncle Jawaharlal elatedly recalled a truncheon battering mounted police had given him during a demonstration against the Simon Commission in 1928.

The sacrificial role had not appealed to the patriarch who had dealt with it characteristically:

> I have nothing to say to your return to wine drinking, if you have (an injured mahatma had written to him on 3 July 1924) but if the report is to be relied on, I cannot but be grieved that you ... should publicly drink and, what is worst, chaff at teetotalism.
>
> The statement, as reported, is too silly even for an after-dinner speech (Motilal Nehru replied). There were many good Muslims at this dinner who drank nothing but pure water. They heartily applauded my remarks and never for a moment dreamt that I was chaffing at teetotalism ... I must express my utter inability to understand how you can possibly reconcile yourself to the suggestion that I might drink privately if at all. I had ... fully made up my mind to revert to total abstinence before the 'prohibition' resolution was moved in the Assembly. But I am going to do nothing of the kind now. I simply cannot bring myself to yield to the puritanism affected in Congress circles ... if there are idiots in the world who still think that, after all I have gone through during the last four years and am going through now, I can be capable of selling my soul to the devil for party purposes, let them think what they like.

The household I remember consisted of grandmother (beaten up herself in a demonstration), great-aunt (the only saint of my acquaintance), the three I thought of as my parents – Ranjit and Vijaya Lakshmi Pandit and Jawaharlal Nehru – besides we three children, cousin Indira being a student in England until she came home to marry in 1942.

There was no mistaking the euphoria. The parents were beautifully, jubilantly in bloom. Jail conditions and the countryside's lung-choking dust played havoc with their health but made for high spirits. I've searched since – it being the fashion – for neurosis, some fearsomely sinister state of mind they might have been hiding, but have come back to the strangeness of their sanity instead. As I bruised my nose on khadi handkerchiefs, sweated over lessons on icebergs, the uses of whale blubber and other features of life on the North Pole, I must have realized the aura they radiated was happiness; and that the world would never be so innocent again.

The cosmopolitan lifestyle, vastly scaled down in a house stripped of extras, continued. The family saw themselves as people of their times and the times had always been complex beside this stretch of the Ganga In the heartland of Hinduism, among the monuments and gardens of Islam, educated as the patriarch had been in Arabic and Persian, his son at Trinity, his son-in-law at Heidelberg, residents of a city whose roads were named after Englishmen, yet was a nerve centre of the national movement, they did not expect to be simple. My father, Ranjit Pandit,. who had translated Kalhana's twelfth century Sanskrit history of Kashmir, *Rajtarangini,* into English, sang 'I want to cling to Ah ha hivy, if Ivy will cling to me' when he shaved. And a custom continued from the splendid days was the governesses. Someone younger than grandmother and great- aunt had to be with us during parental absences. As Indian women did not enter the profession – though one Christian and one Hindu were found for brief periods – they were foreign.

What on earth were these sometimes bewildered white women of the 1930s and '40s doing (and why?) in an Indian family dedicatedly organizing revolt or biding their time in jail until they could? What did they make of such reminders to children as 'We mustn't let the police see us cry,' or letters from jail and elsewhere tenderly exhorting: 'Non-violence is good, my darling. This wise talk about not causing injury, not retaliating, not giving blow for blow is very ancient talk in our country' (letter to the author from Ranjit Pandit, I July 1940). Or 'Prepare yourself to play your part, with a strong body, a sensitive mind that is keen as the edge of a sword and a character that is wedded to high ideals' (letter to the author from Jawaharlal Nehru, 24 November 1942). Whatever their perplexities, they were amazingly at home in the domed house.

Mrs Collins's melancholy repetition of 'I love my husband and my husband loves me' became my first whole English sentence, and convinced grandmother that her husband had deserted her. Mrs Belcher had a heavy smoker's yellow teeth and fingers. Her other addictions were strong tea and superstition. She had me slavishly uncrossing knives, quailing at number 13 and cowering at her story of the voice from the English cemetery croaking, 'I want my buttered toast.' The parents having discarded the shadowy citadel in which part of every Indian lives, regretfully replaced her with a Swiss. But Mademoiselle Colin was eased out when they found us carolling '*Bel fascismo e no salvesta*' from the anthem to II Duce. Miss Ornsholt introduced us to the Viking saga and her side interest, the levitating lamas of Tibet. And when Miss Mills took leave to get her second abortion it was considered prudent not to let her return, though her readings out loud from Wilde and Shaw had been scintillating. Miss Mills, pointing to a picture in the library, of my uncle in his Harrow Rifle Corps uniform, had enlightened a visitor, 'Oh, that's Pandit Nehru when he was in the British army.' Mrs Chew, a Chinese refugee from Singapore, smoked bhang with my best friend's brother to console herself in her exile.

I Hail Maryed at one school, sang 'Yes, Jesus Loves Me' at another, aware that these, like the heroism of Clive and the villainy of the natives, were neither here nor there in the huger, older universe I inhabited at home. Of this my father taught me on walks under the stars, the coolest time to venture out during blistering summers, so that authentic history, including the one the parents were living and theirs had been witness to, was ineluctably linked to the galaxies. I seemed always to be looking up, gazing at their positions in the sky and learning their names along with historic landmarks in the struggle for freedom here on earth.

The Bible gave me no trouble. Its illustrated Jehovah sailed so wrathful and magnificent on clouds high up above the hapless humans huddling below, he could have been grandfather, and uncle the compassionate Christ. Crucifixion and resurrection? They, my father said, were the meaning of what was happening up and down this land. On religion proper I consulted great-aunt and had it from her that Krishna Bhagwan, playing bewitchingly on his flute, or the grand Shiva in tiger skin and ashes, appeared before the true devotee to grant his dearest wish. Mine, just in case, was: Kick out the King. The vision would vanish, my eyes would fly open, and the King would be gone from our stamps. The parents had no such familiarity with the Almighty. Since the patriarch's refusal to perform a purification ceremony on his return from his first voyage overseas, the family had been ostracized by the orthodox. This caused much handed-down hilarity, as did Indians who prospered by British grace and favour, and the pity of the orthodox for us poor children, no dowry, who'd marry us? When the viceroy asked the public to pray for the British Empire and victory against Hitler, my father wrote:

> I was rather far from the Viceroy and was pretty sure he would not notice if I did not pray for the British Empire, nor did I know if God existed. If he does exist, we may be sure he knows what to do with it [letter from Ranjit Pandit, 24 May1940].

The viceroy's God was in any case tainted by the imperial connection, a deity 'beneath whose awful hand we hold/Dominion over palm and pine,' and his appeal a choice piece of irony when he hadn't minded Hitler's rise. The only Providence the family believed in was one that had ordained India to nurture a staggering variety of humanity, and carve out of it a symphony of differences which the world had not yet labelled 'nation'. The national movement, embracing regions, religions, languages, and every racial strain and colour of the human race, was this identity in essence, the mosaic that would constitute nationality.

The parents expected nationalism to disappear when freedom and nationality were ours, as they were sure it must eventually from the face of the earth, for it was not the mystic, inarticulate snarl of blood and gut that Europeans had made it to explain their ferocious tribal wars, or the God-and-Mammon duo of their expansion abroad. Asian sovereignties had never had this dimension of fantasy. A civilized world's borders would be porous, its nations would be geographical, not militant, expressions. After all, when had ordinary people worried about frontiers? Their cattle wandered across them. They loved their fields, streams and forests, and prayed to village gods. Their ultimate national experience was one of being shackled to the same level of primitive subsistence, under a burden of land revenue and debt. Gaining Indian nationality was less about politics, or power (too distant) than about reorganizing society. While every resonant sentence the parents spoke or wrote deconstructed the Empire – which they never doubted would vanish like a pimple off a face – it recreated India a republic of equals, one they themselves might not all live to see. One of them did not, my father contracting pleurisy in jail and dying in 1944 of his last imprisonment.

Their creed, if any, was internationalism. Their involvement with Abyssinia, Spain, China and Czechoslovakia gave notice of the direction foreign policy would take when they had charge, as they seemed instinctively to know they would. They admired America and the Soviet Union for throwing off the feudal yoke and making peerless progress thereafter. They loved jazz and the hour of the Moscow broadcast in English, when my father did his spinning 'so that I can hear of the collective farming of the Soviets while I ply the charkha of Gandhi Baba'! Their canvas was so multifarious, I missed out on dogma. Not for them one Path, one Book, one ism, the foaming mouth, the trance.

> Communism ... aims at producing a classless society where there are no rich and high and mighty who have all the good things and on the other hand a vast mass of ill-clad, ill-fed,

> ill-housed humanity. (Look at the contrast between the rich mill owners of Cawnpore, Bombay and Ahmedabad and their miserable 'mill hands'.) But between theory and practice there is a world of difference. You know the Sermon on the Mount and what a Christian should be like. Now watch the Christian English, French and Germans. And watch the Nazis and Communists tearing up the body of sorely stricken Poland, bravely fighting against overwhelming odds [letter to the author from Ranjit Pandit, 19 September 1939].

Edgar Snow, John Gunther, Eve Curie and others brought us the outside world. Historian Edward Thompson became a friend whose schoolboy son, Palmer (E.P. Thomson), my uncle sometimes wrote to. British Quakers and American missionaries were among those who backed freedom for India. We didn't just sit spellbound listening.

My sister, twelve, gravely asked Margaret Sanger: 'Don't you think. we're well spaced!' and Mrs Sanger, who had failed to enthuse Mahatma Gandhi with contraception for the masses, was charmed.

Asia from which European conquest had isolated us – cutting off ancient sea routes, opening up routes to serve Europe's insatiable appetites – represented more to the family than kinship and culture. On a world stage where everything not Greek in origin was more or less barbarian, where salvation was Jerusalem and glory meant Rome, they projected a faith whose highlights of intellect, aspiration and embattled peasant courage were Asian.

They were confident inter-Asian problems would find wise, mature solutions. Was this how 'the subject races coped with the ruthless destruction of their economies, the falsification of their histories, the imposition of Europe's gun-barrel view? Did their yearning invent an Asia to match Europe's myth of superiority?

Did the family invent the entire world? Theirs would not have fallen apart after the war, leaving its people at the mercy of two terrifyingly armed blocks and now one. Its borders, far from becoming porous, froze. Even as West Europe moved towards unity, invisible barbed wire and broken glass proclaimed For Europeans Only, while tiny murderous nationalisms splintered the East. No just or generous order was established. The market to be served was still somewhere else. The ocean depths and sky were part of it. To go your way left you behind in a race you had no wish to join, whose ultimatum was: Join or die. Did we come all this way, I hear the family ask, to get baited, hooked and fried all over again?

They would have mourned the renaming of Leningrad, and been surprised by the demolition of a church whose message, along with Gandhi's, had made them as invincible as they were.

Now that it had repented of its tyrannies and seen the light, by what rationale did communism deserve to be trashed when, the evil deeds of other religions notwithstanding, religion was still in use?

The collapse of basic assumptions about their own republic would have appalled them. In their own, somehow prescient, 'tryst with destiny', they never foresaw the bloody combine of religious, ethnic and secessionist savagery that would butcher, among thousands of others, two whose calculatedly shredded remains would hardly make respectable corpses for their state funerals.

But had they known they would have insisted the proposition that is 'India' is our most civilized achievement in six thousand years, not to be destroyed by any variation of the foaming mouth, the trance. If they were told it's happening everywhere, countries are fracturing, there's only one ism now, and it's carnival time for fanatics, they would repeat:

But friends and comrades, this is India. Hold on.

Admittedly the view from the domed house, and its India, were strange for their sanity.

Statement in the United Nations General Assembly*

Mr President,

It is a great honour for me, on behalf of the government and people of India, and as the niece of Jawaharlal Nehru, to receive this award to Pandit Nehru for his contribution to the struggle against apartheid.

Nehru devoted his life to India's fight for freedom from imperial domination, but it was a struggle intimately connected, for him, with the urge towards freedom and dignity in other parts of the world, and more especially in support of those who laboured under, and daily experienced, the scourge of apartheid. His resolute stand against racism was no mere academic matter, nor even merely the hallmark of a civilized man's conscience. As part of mankind's non-white majority, he profoundly resented this insult to the human spirit, and the evil effects of such a policy upon vast numbers of men, women and children. He opposed racial discrimination with his intellect, his emotion and his passion. He called it 'the greatest international immorality' and when he spoke of it in the Indian Parliament, he deplored moderation on this issue. 'It surprises

* Statement by Mrs Nayantara Saghal, Representative of India, in the special meeting of the General Assembly to observe the international anti-apartheid year on 11 October 1978 on acceptance of award to Jawaharlal Nehru

me,' he said on one occasion, 'that countries, particularly those who stand for the democratic tradition and those who voted for the United Nations Charter and the International Convention on Human Rights, express themselves so moderately, or do not express themselves at all, about the racial policy of the South African Union.' For him there was no question of counselling patience, moderation or compromise in the face of this continuing affront to human dignity.

The people of India have had a long involvement with the struggle against apartheid, Mahatma Gandhi played a courageous and pioneering role in this struggle at the turn of the century when he organized and led non-violent resistance in South Africa against the regime's unjust and discriminatory laws. Independent India carried the struggle forward by breaking off all relations with South Africa in protest against racist policies. Under Nehru's leadership India brought the issue of apartheid in South Africa to the General Assembly, and it was my mother Mrs Vijaya Lakshmi Pandit's proud privilege to present it at the very first session of the United Nations in 1946. In 1952, India together with twelve Asian and Arab countries warned the United Nations that a race conflict in South Africa, resulting from the policy of apartheid, would become a threat to world peace, a view that was widely accepted in the General Assembly nine years later. The credit for this achievement goes to the Special Committee against Apartheid and particularly to the dynamic leadership provided by Nigeria as its chairman. Yet we know that effective action is yet to be taken against a defiant member who persists in what the General Assembly has called a crime against humanity. The fight against apartheid is entering a critical phase. It must be fought to the finish if the efforts of those whom we honour here today, and the sufferings of many who live under its intolerable conditions, are not to have been in vain. My country pledges its continued and full support to the struggle until final victory.

Thank you, Mr President.

PART SEVEN

Reminders of a Cherished Friendship

Letters from E.P. Thompson and Dorothy Norman

124 East 70th Street
New York 21, NY
5 April 1954

Dearest Tara,

You are an angel. Your book* is lovely. I am happy to have read it. I hope it is a success.

How are you? *I think of you so often.* This is just a quick note, so that it may reach you In the greatest haste. I wanted to communicate with you. *I think of you so often.* With such tenderness. I wish we could meet. I doubt whether I shall ever get to India again, somehow.

Are you planning to come to the West? Are you going on with your writing? I have a longing to hear about you, to know about you. And to send you my love.

Always devotedly,
Dorothy

---

* *Prison and Chocolate Cake*

I July 1986

Dear Nayantara Sahgal,

Oh dear, oh dear, my head is covered with ashes – it is now 8 months since you wrote to me. I had written to thank you for *Rich Like Us* and told you that I liked it: this was true, but it was also a half-fib, since I had only read one-third of it then (which I liked). My daughter Kate had then nabbed it and carried it off to Ireland (she is our India expert, having spent two years bumming around – and even doing some useful work – in India). So when you wrote to invite me to send a line, it was in the Republic, County Clare, and I had long negotiations to get it back. Then my time disappeared into the black hole of the peace movement for some months, as it has been doing for the past seven years when I cannot call my life my own. The result is that I only finished reading it three weeks ago.

It is a superb, beautifully crafted, searching and compassionate book – a very remarkable book, from which I learned a great deal, and which at the same time thrust one into authentic problems whose resolution goes far beyond easy programmes or pat political programmatic. I do thank you so much for your insight. I thank you also for your charity towards that muddle which was British India. (A charity which may make some – who wrap up all history in holdalls like 'imperialism' and 'racism' – regard you critically). I thank you also for the constructive 'feminism': it seems to me that certain writers – you and Nadine Gordimer – who are writing about whole human situations are so much more effective than trendy Western stridencies. The flashbacks to 'sati' were moving and effective. It is one of the very few books of our times which will last.

I'm sorry that I'm too late to write a line for the dust jacket, but it is a book that I shall hand around and recommend. My wife Dorothy is now into it and is already hooked.

In little intervals from peace chores I've been much preoccupied with 'India' this last few months.

Indian scholars (not British) trek here to look at my father's papers. I got involved in a 125th Tagore Festival and have been working on these papers myself, writing up a lecture. One day I might even write an essay on the Nehru relation. But any fuller study must be from other hands. What comes through to me chiefly is the complexity of the cultural relation. I get *furious* with all the youngsters now who think that all that needs to be known is imperialism and racism and who have these holdall terms like Third World and 'blacks' which supposedly contain the most diverse cultural and social exchanges. It is a sort of 'Left paternalism' mixed with guilt.

If you are in England again please give us a little more notice – we would love you to come here. I would like to show you some papers – or if you are pressed for time we could run down to London – or 'Babylon' as my father used to call Calcutta.

Very good wishes,
Yours sincerely,
Edward Thompson

24 July 1986

Dear Nayantara Sahgal,

Thanks so much for your letter. By the way, I'm not a professor. That is a libel imposed upon me by the media. In fact since 1971 I've been a self-employed writer and unpaid agitator. I only get to being a 'professor' when I visit places as a visiting prof., like USA and India.

In the middle of October I shall be hiding on a Welsh mountain and trying to finish a book. We shall be here at the beginning and end. Lots of room, big house.

I wonder if you know my friend, Sumit Sarkar, a professor of history at Delhi University? He has written a long introduction to a new edition of my father's *On the Other Side of the Medal.* He kindly sent the draft to me for comment, and I disagreed with a passing reference to my father's *Suttee,* in which he seemed to place it alongside *Mother India.* I started thinking about the problem and in the course of it did a little more reading, so I sent Sumit a note on that question. I'm sure he won't mind if I send you a copy. I am a complete duffer about the whole thing, but your own treatment of it is most moving.

Can you tell your daughter that Kate had a baby (her second) last week. A second daughter.

Yours sincerely,
Edward Thompson

N. Wales, 16 September 1986

Dear Mrs Sahgal,

Sorry to be so slow in writing, wanted to read *Plans for Departure* first, which have been doing in Wales. It is so beautifully written: too whimsical to move one as much as *Rich Like Us,* but a lovely entertainment. Yes, it wouldn't go down with main-line literary folk on US east or west coast, who wouldn't know which bits were funny (not that I was always sure).

I have always been interested in this thing about American sense of humour – they *do* have a sense of humour, but it is dead in a whole range. I have thought that Americans could never understand 'Indians' because of this, but 'we' somehow can share the same sense of humour. That is not as true as it was. 'We' both used to share a similar taste in irony. My father wrote about this several times, with reference to Bengali writing. But nowadays I find it very dangerous to write anything ironical. Not only is it (a) always misunderstood by Americans and (b) untranslatable but (c) most English readers under thirty don't read it either. They are so full up with slapstick pseudo-satire (*Private Eye* and Auberon Waugh invective and *Spitting Image*) that they are insensitized.

All August I was performing a filial duty I never expected, writing up 100 plus pages of a study of my father and Bengal literary circles from 1913 to 1922. (I am a bit of an expert now on one or two of the signals you refer to in 1913-14, I fact I'm not 100 per cent sure you've got all of them right.) I would like to ask you to read this.

Amazing the things I find in my attic. (Like all those letters of Anna's*.) I share with you the decidedly unpopular view that there was something on the margins of the British Indian experience which still rewards study and meditation – something quite considerable and refusing to lie down and go dead – but this is very much not the flavour-of-the-month, least of all in radical circles, who would prefer to put it all into categories and stereotypes. Like blacks, imperialism and hegemony.

My father had an awful runaround from the Tagore clique and if it hadn't been for Prashanta and Rani Mahalanobis the whole episode would have turned rancid. But they redeemed it. And redeemed the greatness of Tagore.

In regard to the said attic, do please *identify* yourself. I keep finding out that some of my Calcutta friends turn out to be nephews or grandchildren of my father's own circle. If I can establish your *genealogy* I may even turn up some letters from your own kin in my attic.

Which is to say it would be very nice if you could spare at the least a full day with us in Worcester, so that we can investigate the said attic together. If that's not possible, Dorothy and I would love to run down to London and have a meal with you. But it would be nice for us if you and Gita (and your husband, if he likes attics) could come up to us. Logistics: I am immersed in preaching peace 1 to 4 October, and sundry German and US visitors are descending during 4–8. Shortly after that I hope to escape back here to N. Wales to do some essential writing for about two weeks. Back in Worcester by 25 (Sunday). Any time suits me. Sunday (25) – there is a good morning train – to Tuesday (27) or Wednesday. The date 28 October is good, and the following weekend, 31 October to 2 November, is OK also, if you are still in England. Maybe you could ring between 4 and 8 October to Worcester? If my dates don't suit you I could postpone my flight to the Welsh mountains. Dorothy will be at Worcester when I am away and you could sort it out on the phone.

Sincerely,
Edward Thompson

---

* a character in *Plans for Departure*

27 October 1986

Dear Nayantara,

It was so lovely to see you. It felt like the closing of a figure of eight.

And Gita is *super*. Maybe there is a little hope for the world. Wouldn't it be nice to think that our children's children might still have something which made them friends?

Devi Prasad (whom I mentioned) published a book on Peace Education or Education for Peace. (Gandhi Peace Foundation, New Delhi). He is a gentle-mannered man and, I think, a strict Gandhian pacifist.

I enclose, for your light reading, my reply to the British Council. I've sent copies of the dossier to historian friends (Sumit Sarkar, Barun De) in case they are in need of a laugh. I've told them to publish it in 'Calcutta Comic Cuts'.

I feel I need 1987 for a really straight spell of my own historical writing. If my 'Gulliver' makes any money (with my Rani wedded according to proper synthetic rites) then I very much hope that I — and Dorothy – will be able to come to India in late 1988 or in 1989, under our own auspices and not beholden to any stuffy Council.

'Great thing of no forget' – Nayantara, I did not send with you any gift or message for your mother. Could you kindly repair my oversight? Please convey my profound admiration and tell her that a few of us here still remember the true traditions of Congress and teach our children and our students.

I cannot at this short notice think of anything appropriate to send. Perhaps she would like this late lecture of my father's – one of the last public lectures he delivered? And did you take a copy of the enclosed letter? From Padmaja Naidu? And the 'aerogram' from your mother?

I send a copy of the lecture inscribed to Gandhi. In the conditions of the war it could not be sent, and at the end of the war my father was already very ill with cancer. He writes about your uncle on pages 29-36.

With warm wishes from us both to both of you,
Edward

3 December 1986

Dear Nayantara,

Excuse a hurried typed note. I am off to Ireland tomorrow and haven't written my lectures yet.

Lovely to get your long letter and enclosures. This is just to say that the high commissioner rang me twice, to persuade me to come to a very posh governmental conference of VIP's in New Delhi on 11–16 January. It is in memory of Indira. I just wasn't sure whether to go or not and how our Indian friends will regard it – I tried to ring Gita for advice, but couldn't get her. In the end I said 'yes'. I shall just be in and out, and presumably confined to some conference complex. Will try and make a proper visit in 1988 or 1989.

I'll try and write a proper letter later.

Warmest wishes,
Edward

12-16 January 1987

Dear Nayantara,

Being in India for this week I must send a note to apologize for not getting in touch – it all happened unexpectedly and swiftly, first the British Council stopping me, and then the Indian high commissioner urging me to come. I didn't know if it was right to come or not. (I tried to consult Gita by phone but could never get her.) The conference is at the highest level of generality, and too much rhetoric. I played truant yesterday, visiting Delhi University and seeing old friends. I also have spent a pleasant evening with the Kumars. Today all the delegates are invited to lunch with Rajiv. I have never been in such a rarefied atmosphere. My contribution to the rhetoric was to propose moving the UN from New York to New Delhi – but I'm not sure the Indian people would benefit from a new layer of spies, terrorists and bureaucrats.

I never properly responded to your earlier letter. I liked your article (and of course if you ever have anything we could copy in *EN-Journal*, please let me know.) The story 'Martand' is moving – but it seems to me to be suggesting more than could possibly be said in a story so short. It is almost a synopsis for a novel.

We are well and Dorothy sends greetings. Hard at work. Better things really do seem to be happening in the Soviet Union. It is lovely to be in India again, even if in the strange surroundings of hotels and conference halls – quite determined that we must both come back for a proper visit in 1988.

With warmest wishes,
Edward

9 June 1987

Dear Nayantara,

That is so kind of you and I do enclose a CV (which is academic and does not really cover political questions nor the work of the peace movement 1980 on) but also you *must not do* this. And among other reasons, I have been seriously ill this year – ulcerative colitis – especially in February-April, and I am still under a dosage of steroids and the doctor says I shouldn't travel until I am right again. So that if the Nehru Award* came my way I almost certainly couldn't come to India in 1987 to receive it – which would look rude. What I'm hoping to do is get my health back and then maybe Dorothy and I could spend some weeks in India – visiting universities and friends – in 1989! But the health thing is a serious problem.

Good to hear from you and good to hear about your novel. Have you seen Praful Bidwai's articles (in *Times of India*) on nuclear questions – they seem good to me.

Dorothy joins in greetings.

Edward

* My mother had, at my suggestion, proposed E.P. Thompson's name for the Nehru Award for International Understanding.

2 July 1987

Dear Nayantara,

I am enclosing copies of various (mostly a little out of date) writings on India and nuclear weapons. Praful B. is very good.

You are very kind but *please* don't push my name. I really do seem to be making a very slow recovery. I am still on those steroids which are most depressing and I just don't know when I'll be able to travel freely – or if. I can't put two thoughts together.

We should be here in late August but we might possibly be in Wales.

We have just had a visit from Dharma Kumar, a very forceful personality!

Dorothy joins in good wishes.

Edward

27 June 1988

Dear Nayantara.

We got back from Canada a week or two ago to find a mountain of mail. A quick sort-through, and we put aside some things to come back to, like leaving the icing from the cake until last, when the boring and choring had been dealt with. So it was only yesterday evening that I finally settled down to read your book* and only then discovered the dedication. We are both honoured and delighted by it, and shall be reading the book with a sense of possession as well as pleasure.

One of the reasons for dashing back from the other side of the Atlantic was the publication of Edward's novel; and one of the chores that has been holding us up has been getting copies for him to inscribe for special friends. There is one for you among these, and Edward is very apologetic about the delay in sending it. But things have been extremely hectic since we got back, tomorrow we dash off to Sweden for a few days for the E.N.D. Convention, next weekend Edward has to be in Oxford, but then, at last, we shall have a couple of months at home.

I am not sure where this should be sent to, or whether you are in Britain, India or the U.S. If the former, do think of us if you have any free weekends. We'd love to see you here.

Again, very many thanks for the dedication, and very best wishes from us both.

Affectionately,
Dorothy

---

* *Mistaken Identity*

27 August 1988

Dear Nayantara,

Such a great honour – and I have been so slow to write! The fact is that I am still only half well, and so slow with everything.

Yes, I do like *Mistaken Identity* very much, although in the first quarter I wasn't sure that I was going to. Well, this is true of all your novels – those I've read – a sense of some indecision early on and then growing definition and confidence leading to a triumphantly controlled second half. I think this may be an effect of your careful pre-plotting? That is, you decide that there are certain things (which you know and the characters know) which you won't tell the readers until later in the book. You do this in *Plans For Departure* but it is so much the case in *Mistaken Identity* that the reader might feel that you were manipulating him. As in pages 88-90 versus page 168 where you seem to give different accounts? In short, in the first section I thought the narrative was 'managed' too much as a literary device – and it was some time before I could altogether accept the credibility of Bhushan Singh. He also seemed to be a literary device, a neutral camera, able to record any cultural situation – including his mother's – that you wished to enter.

But my reservations grew less and less as I went on, and the second half of the book is amazingly successful, light-footed, wry, most moving through its understatement and its tangential address to heroic themes which have become weary and cliched from their bombastic rhetorical reiteration. To use Bhushan Singh as a kind of

Candide or Idiot or Holy Fool is a marvellous foil to all the other characters. He enables you to present tragic issues in a downbeat, half-comic way which gives your book a unique quality and a feeling more authentic than a heavy tragic or heroic mode.

Anyway, thank you again. Dorothy and I are proud of the dedication.

We are going to New Zealand for the last three weeks of September – I am lecturing in Auckland – and then I have a research fellowship at Manchester for a year. That is, I shall be paid for doing what I would be doing anyway – finishing my next history book – but will have to shuttle between Worcester (at weekends) and Manchester.

The annoying thing is that while I'm better I'm still not fully recovered, and perhaps never will be.

However, I've at least been taken off the worst part of the medication (steroids) for a trial period, so I'm hoping to get back more mental energy. I've done almost *nothing* of writing for eighteen months. Reception of *Sykaos Papers* mixed, as if everyone has read a different book. Serious 'middle' reviews have been kind (*Observer* and *Sunday Times*), but the modish London Left very hostile (*New Statesman, Private Eye*) – I am *not* the flavour of the month in that quarter. Nor wish to be.

I'm sorry we didn't see you when you passed through London last year. Don't let it happen again.

I hope there's good news of Gita. We seem to have lost sight of her. Radha Kumar is in England just now, taking a course at Brighton. We had a nice visit from her.

Edward

18 March 1989

Dear Nayantara,

You couldn't have sent me a nicer letter about *Sykaos Papers*,* although I'm sad that it depressed you. Yes, some of it was depressing to write. But I had finished it before I became ill, or before I knew that I was ill. And much of it I enjoyed writing in 'our' cottage on a mountain in Wales, looking out at the night sky. I can reassure you about the final pages and Ho Mo. He *escapes* in a little spaceship, with an Eve, and was intending to fly back to the blue planet. So there is a sequel still to be written one day. In truth I feel a bit lonely without the book to write.

Mind you, I think I made one big mistake. I ought to have left it much more *indefinite* what happened to Sykaro. It would have been easy to have contrived the Pitariane to fly back home leaving the fate of Sykaro quite undecided. This would have left more for the reader's imagination to work on.

I see that Gorbachev got the Peace prize and I'm truly delighted. There has been a quite extraordinary change in the prospects of the world since G started his initiatives – I feel much more hopeful than a few years ago. But the situation is still very

* *The Sykaos Papers* is a novel by E.P. Thompson, published by Bloomsbury, 1988

tense. British politicians go on with their tit for tats and have made no response.

We are going to do a last stint of teaching in the USA next academic year, at Rutgers, New Jersey This means we shall leave for USA about 10 or 15 August. So if you are coming to the conference try and spend some time in England *before* it and pay us a visit here.

My health is not too bad – 'stabilized' – but I must follow your advice and take up yoga. My daughter Kate is always telling me this – she is a qualified yoga teacher.

Dorothy sends her love and we both hope that the new novel is going well.

With warm regards,
Edward

222 South Second Avenue
Holland Park, New Jersey 08904 USA
26 October 1989

Dear Nayantara,

I was distressed to learn that your mother is seriously ill. I have heard nothing and am anxious.

Please give her my kindest wishes.

We shall be here until June. So if you are to be in USA, please let us know. It is an easy trip to New York. As I get older I wish to spend more time seeing friends!

My health has been terrible here. In fact I am writing from hospital. But I shall be out and about very soon.

The *work* (teaching) is good. Good students. The intellectual climate is *terrible* – flaky decadence especially among the pseudo-radicals. All ego fulfilment and self-privileging strategies. The *pay* is very good. It is like working in a silver mine and will keep us from having to sell our house for two or three more years.

We *must* admire what Gita is doing.

Love from us both

Edward

PS. *Mistaken Identity* keeps on growing in my mind. It really is rich.

29 January 1991

Dear Nayantara,

Thank you for your kind letter. We must try to catch you this time when you are in England. I have not been as far afield as London yet, but I am confident that I shall be able to in March. So if you cannot come as far as Worcester, we shall do our best to come to London. We have some friends in London who would I am sure lend us space in their house in St Johns Wood to make tea, and we could go out for a meal.

The Gulf War is absurd. I cannot be pro-Hussein, his regime is so foul, but the Americans continue to refuse any way to a negotiated settlement. Some of them clearly *wanted* this outcome to secure the oil and to imprint their hegemony on western Asia. The American people appear to be protesting quite vigorously.

Dorothy sends love. We'll expect you to ring from London.

Edward

4 February 1992

Dear Nayantara,

Yes, indeed, I got your earlier letter about my brother and I should have written to thank you long ago. Delay is partly due to my permanent invalid state, aggravated by a mild pneumonia during January. My lungs are seriously impaired and won't improve, and I fall victim to any infection going. My doctor won't let me travel anywhere, not even to London, in the winter.

I'm sorry you've had such a bad year – it must have been awful. And it is quite absurd that a novelist of your distinction should be looking for a publisher. I hope that is no longer the case.

No, your *Guardian* piece on nationalism hasn't appeared yet.

I can get to my desk and potter on with my study of 'Contexts for William Blake'. I am wrestling with Swedenborg now, which is enough to make anyone confused. Dorothy is in good health and doing some vigorous winter gardening. We are going into the most empty and opportunist general election of my lifetime – we have *no* respect for the Labour Party, whose only policy is 'We want office on any terms'. I am not much inspired by Russian intellectuals – an abject collapse.

What is your admirable daughter up to?

Very warm wishes from us both,

Edward

3 October 1993

Dear Nayantara,

Thank you so much for your letter.

Edward died suddenly and peacefully in the sunny garden. He was working at his desk until the day before, and never became really dependent. So although there was a lot more he would have done if his health had not been broken, he did have a very full life until the end, and did complete most of the major projects he had in mind. The Blake book will be in the shops in a few weeks. I have had a pre-publication copy already, and he had sent off a collection of historical essays a couple of days before he died.

Edward greatly valued our friendship with you – you and your work have helped us so much to find some keys to the England–India connection.

With love,
Dorothy